SO-BEE-841

#035

I WANT TO Make Money in the Stock Market

A step-by-step process you can follow to enter the fascinating world of Stock Market investing.

Learn to begin investing without losing your life savings.

Chris M. Hart, Sr.

May everything you lay your
hand to prosper!

Outskirts Press, Inc.
Denver, Colorado

MJ

The opinions expressed in this manuscript are solely the opinions of the author and do not represent the opinions or thoughts of the publisher. The author represents and warrants that s/he either owns or has the legal right to publish all material in this book. If you believe this to be incorrect, contact the publisher through its website at www.outskirtspress.com.

I WANT TO Make Money in the Stock Market
Learn to begin investing without losing your life savings!
All Rights Reserved

Copyright © 2005 Chris M. Hart, Sr.

This book may not be reproduced, transmitted, or stored in whole or in part by any means, including graphic, electronic, or mechanical without the express written consent of the publisher except in the case of brief quotations embodied in critical articles and reviews.

Outskirts Press
http://www.outskirtspress.com

ISBN-10: 1-59800-206-6
ISBN-13: 978-1-59800-206-5

Library of Congress Control Number 2005935912

Outskirts Press and the "OP" logo are trademarks belonging to
Outskirts Press, Inc.

Printed in the United States of America

What others are saying about this book

"Chris Hart's writing style and humorous examples made reading this book a pleasure. I have surprised myself that I really understand and can apply the concepts I learned from him! I hope he will continue to write how-to books."

"At last, a book on investing for the rest of us! It is simple and to the point. Thanks for teaching us how to "...Make Money in the Stock Market" without making us feel like we are studying to become CPAs."

"The step-by-step format of <u>I WANT TO Make Money in the Stock Market</u> gives you the tools and confidence necessary to take on today's stock market."

"I had no prior investing experience. After reading this book, I feel confident about diving into the stock market and becoming a "Student of Commerce." It really broke the process down into terms anyone can relate to no matter what level of expertise they have."

"This book can truly change your life by providing techniques and strategies you can use to develop and monitor your own investments."

"Anyone who is "stuck" financially, but who diligently takes the time to apply the strategy you provide, can transform his or her future. For many people on marginal incomes, this may be the key that unlocks the door to financial stability and then financial abundance. That would be awesome!!"

CONTENTS AT A GLANCE

TABLE OF CONTENTS

TABLE OF FIGURES

This book is dedicated to my beautiful wife, Donna, whose ever-present smile and constant encouragement lead me to believe that I can do anything!

PREFACE

The Stock Market...Haven't you always wondered what it really is? Maybe you have yearned for the "special" knowledge your friends who are "in" the stock market seem to have. Maybe you have known someone who "made a fortune" in the stock market and that intrigued you. Maybe you asked yourself, "If they made money, can I?" Or, quite possibly, maybe you know someone who "lost a bunch of money" in the stock market and that scared you...but you still want to know more about this mythical beast or you wouldn't have this book in your hands.

If any of the above apply to you, then you're in the same position I was several years ago. I was fascinated by news reports of the stock market reaching new highs and then having "corrections." I wanted to know more. I wanted to understand. I wanted to **be** one of those "special" people who understood this great American institution well enough to participate. But I didn't have a clue where to begin. So, I started a quest. I set out to learn. I began to read books and search Internet sites about the stock market.

I found that there are hundreds of books about stock market investing. Most of them are written by experts and professionals with years of great experience as professional stockbrokers, financial advisors, certified tax lawyers, IRS agents, bankers, and seasoned business people. However, I knew virtually nothing about investing and the stock market. I needed to start with the very basics and then know exactly what to do every step of the way. I started my quest, determined to self-teach myself the skills necessary to start investing. I observed and studied the market for two years before I made my first trade. I am convinced that I could have started investing much sooner if I would have had THIS book. THIS is the book I wish I had when I was trying to figure out:

- What exactly IS the stock market?

- How do I get started?

- How do I keep from losing my life savings?

Why I want you to have this book

Through study and trial and error, I have had a very satisfying experience learning to be a stock market investor. I have seen the value of my portfolio increase and have NOT lost my life savings! So, to sum up why I want you to have this book, I'll borrow part of the book's title:

I WANT TO explain exactly what the stock market is and how you can participate

I WANT TO give you a step-by-step tutorial on how to begin investing

I WANT TO point out the risks of investing in the stock market and design strategies to minimize those risks

I WANT TO show you how to be a confident investor who knows how to protect your assets while watching them grow

This book is written in plain, every-day language and will allow you to begin your experience as a stock market investor right away. With this book as your guide, I believe that you will also find this journey to be exciting and rewarding. Now...let's get started!

PART ONE

In Part One you will learn

- Why you are the best person to direct your investments

- How the Internet will enable you to have the same power tools used by professional investors

- Why you'll like investing in stocks more than other financial instruments

- How to never be a victim of risk but to **use** risk to increase your rewards

- How to fit successful investing in with a full life, career, and family

- Which tools you will need to start investing

- Different types of brokerage accounts and which one is right for you

- Where you can get the money to start your investing fund.

1

Am I Smart Enough to Invest in the Stock Market?

Have you ever wondered why all the stockbrokers in the world aren't rich?

Whatever you don't know about can seem mysterious, difficult, and complicated. Stockbrokers spend all day "IN" the stock market, whatever IN is. Therefore, if you're uninformed about how to invest in the stock market, stockbrokers can seem like possessors of secret, magic knowledge. Furthermore, we could form the opinion that they alone have the difficult skills required to navigate the treacherous labyrinths of buying and selling stocks. If this is the opinion we have of stockbrokers, then it begs the question – "Why aren't they all rich?"

The fact of the matter is that the average salary for a typical stockbroker in the United States is $48,689! The point is this: stockbrokers are hard-working professionals who offer financial services to the public. However, you are not required to use their services in order to invest in the stock market and receive handsome returns on your investments. You can do what they do. In fact, you can do it better! Why?

It's YOUR Hard-Earned Money

Nobody will be as interested in protecting and growing your Hard-Earned Money as you will be.

A stockbroker's objective is to sell enough financial services to earn their average $48k per year. Your objective is to invest your Hard-Earned Money, **protect it from loss,** and make a profit. Right?

A stockbroker is looking after the money of how many people? Maybe dozens. You are looking after the money of how many people? One. Just yours. How bad does a stockbroker feel if your investment loses money? Not very. It's not his money.

How bad do YOU feel when your investment loses money? Terrible! That was YOUR Hard-Earned Money! If you have a loss, you're going to analyze what went wrong, learn from it, and work hard at not letting it happen again. Investing on your own will require you to learn some new skills and invest time as well as money.

Why should I work to invest my own Hard-Earned Money in the stock market?

There are several reasons:

- It's satisfying to study something, calculate the risk, make a decision, and then see the result.

- The stockbroker's motivation is not the same as yours. His is to get your money into his hands. Yours is to keep and grow your money.

- There are many areas of life that you cannot control. Learning the skills to do your own investing is an area you CAN control and master. And, you can do it much quicker than you may think. Hold on, Future Stock Market Investor...you're about to become a Student of Commerce!

"The universe is full of magical things patiently waiting for our wits to grow sharper."

Eden Phillpotts (1862-1960) Indian-born British Novelist

Definition of Student

- One who is being educated: a learner, pupil or scholar.

- One who studies something: "a student of contemporary dance."

- One who is an attentive observer: "a student of world affairs."

- One who is a learned person: someone who by long study has gained mastery in one or more disciplines.

Definition of Commerce

- Commerce is the buying and selling of goods.

- Commerce is done between businesses, individuals, or countries.

- Commerce is the exchange of something of value between two entities. That "something" may be goods, services, information, money, or anything else the two entities consider to have value.

- Commerce is the central mechanism from which capitalism is derived.

This book will be your step-by-step guide on how to actually start investing in the stock market. You will also want to study some of the other vast resources available on the subject. The more you know about the stock market and investing, the better an investor you will be. So, yes, this book will get you started, but it's **your** job to become a Student of Commerce.

Does the word "student" make you uncomfortable?

It shouldn't. Even if you had a less than stellar experience in school, you have the ability now to be a GREAT student. See, this time, it's on **your** terms. This time, **you** are the boss! You are going to be learning a subject that will propel you into a universe of fascinating knowledge and information. You are choosing to educate yourself. Therefore, you will study **what** you want **when** you want to. And, instead of a grade on a piece of paper, your rewards will be very tangible. Money, confidence, and self-satisfaction are just a few.

Do I have to go to class?

Absolutely! The great news is that the classroom will be wherever and whenever you want it to be. You'll get to wear whatever you choose, and you can have pink hair if you want. You'll be creating a virtual classroom. Many times, you'll be studying and learning as you go through your daily routine of life. Watching the news, reading the newspaper, talking to friends...they all have the opportunity to educate you as a Student of Commerce.

Where do I get the curriculum?

Since you're interested in investing and in the stock market, you will now begin to hear of news stories and hallway conversations that catch your interest. Here's a starting point for resources to which you can expose yourself:

- Brick and mortar bookstores and libraries

Visit any of the excellent retail bookstores or public libraries and look in the following sections:

> Investing, Online Investing, Internet Investing

> Business

> Stocks, Stock Market

> Finance, Financial Markets, Personal Finance

> Securities

> Day Trading

I don't suggest you consider Day Trading until you have a great deal of experience successfully investing. However, reading a book on the subject will help you understand many of the related subjects better.

- Online bookstores

Visit your favorite online bookstores and look under the same categories as listed above for the brick and mortar bookstores. Good online bookstores will allow you to enter keywords and will then display a list of books that address the keyword subject. You can visit www.ChrisHart1.com for a listing of top online bookstores.

- Online resources and websites

Throughout this book, I will suggest that you do an "Internet search" to locate online resources. If you would like help on how to do an effective Internet search, visit www.ChrisHart1.com. There you will find a listing of top search engines as well as tips on how to make your search more productive. Pull up your favorite search engine and look up the following words:

- ➤ Stock market investing

- ➤ Stock portfolio

- ➤ Picking stocks

Entering the word combinations above will give you hundreds of links to follow. You'll quickly see other subjects on which to search. I do this every so often because there are new sites being added every day. You can study the site's info as you search, or you can add the site to your favorites list to read later.

- Television

  - ➤ Financial reports on the network news

  - ➤ Channels dedicated to financial and stock market issues (usually on cable)

- Locker room banter

Sure! Go ahead! Join in with the guys or gals when they're talking about their investments. Listen to what they're doing. See how they pick stocks. They may have some techniques that you can study and add to your knowledge arsenal. On the other hand, they may be shooting in the dark. They may **not** have dedicated themselves to being Students of Commerce like you have. In fact, you may need to do them a favor and suggest that they buy a copy of this book so that they can have the benefit of learning these basic skills like you have!

The Internet – How you will level the playing field

The Internet is a wonderfully powerful tool that will put in your hands the same capability that professional investors have. To better understand how online investing has developed in the last few years, let's take a glimpse back into recent history. Back in the olden days of the 20ᵗʰ century, a stock market investor's activities were very different from what yours will be. First of all, very few people researched and purchased individual stocks. Here's why...

To learn about the performance of stocks, the main source of information was printed on paper. Big books containing a history of stock prices were available in public libraries, but were usually several months old. You could spend hours flipping through pages, squinting at the tiny print, and scribbling your notes on a pad. Once you found some stocks you thought might be good investment candidates, you would probably come back to the library a couple more times to check the next month's publication to see how they were doing.

When you were ready to buy stocks, the fastest way was to pick up the phone and call your stockbroker. You would have a live conversation with him or her about what you wanted to buy. Since these were all "full-service brokers," they were compelled to give you advice on your requested purchase and recommend other stocks they thought you should invest in. Then, depending on what you decided to buy, the stockbroker would place the order for you. The order could go in as quickly as within the hour, but might not be executed until the next business day. Wondering about the cost of this very time-consuming transaction? Anywhere from $50 to $200 or more!

In order to purchase individual stocks, most people simply didn't want to spend that much time to get so little data that cost so much.

Consequently, they relied on full-service stockbrokers to advise them on which stocks would be best for them. These full-service stockbrokers were not evil people. It's just that the market system was set up so that they got paid a commission for every stock they sold **and** for every stock they bought. So, whether or not **you** made money on your stock transaction, **they did**. In addition, they were often offered incentives for selling certain stocks. As you can see, the system was set up to favor **their** income, not

yours. Then, something happened that changed the course of history in the universe!

A technical revolution

By the late 1980s, Personal Computers (PCs) had become powerful enough to be a serious desktop tool. At the same time, the prices were coming down so that individual consumers could afford them. In the 1990s, this trend continued until PCs were very powerful and very inexpensive. As a result, many people bought them to use in their homes.

Here comes the Web!

The Internet started out as a highly complex network of computers developed in universities to exchange scientific data. As the Internet began to evolve, it was not long until it became easy enough for John and Suzy Q. Public to use, and its momentum built like a tidal wave. In just a few short years, the Internet developed so that not only computers, but virtually every type of digital device made, could be connected to it. The list is endless and includes cell phones, personal digital assistants, refrigerators, home theater systems, vending machines, traffic cameras, and even clothing.

Access to the Internet from a PC has changed the way we are able to get information and make decisions. By the time this book is in print, the entire Library of Congress should be available online. From the comfort of your recliner, you can now access almost all of the published work of modern mankind.

This scenario is vastly different from driving to the library multiple times and spending hours poring over dated, hard-to-read information.

Stockbroker services morph into a new life form

As the world was quickly getting connected via the Internet, the full-service stockbrokers were changing, too. The brokerage houses realized that if they allowed customers to log on to a website and place their own orders, it cost the brokerage services very little. They could still charge a heavily discounted fee for tendering the transaction **and** make money. This concept grew rapidly. Soon all brokerage houses offered online transactions.

The term Online Broker was coined to refer to the service the brokerage house offered whereby **your** computer communicated with **their** computer to execute stock transactions. Soon after the success of Online Brokers at full-service brokerages, brokerage companies were formed that ONLY offered online transactions. With the ability to sit in front of your Personal Computer and extensively study potential investments, and then buy and sell stocks with a few clicks of the mouse, the balance of power shifted dramatically.

Not only can you now gain all the knowledge you need to successfully direct your own investments, you can execute the transactions yourself!

Summary

- You not only ARE smart enough to invest in the stock market, you're getting smarter because you're a Student of Commerce.

- You're the BEST person in the world to invest your money because nobody cares about your Hard-Earned Money as much as you do.

- The Internet is a powerful tool that enables you to study investments and directly execute transactions just like the pros!

2

Is It Gambling to Put Money in the Stock Market?

The title of this chapter is a very good question for both moral and practical reasons. The short answer is, honestly, it could be. Now, before you think too much about why you bought a book on gambling, let me tell you this:

I DO NOT believe in gambling for BOTH moral and practical reasons!

In fact, one of the very basic objectives of this book is to educate you so that you are NOT gambling your money. I want to teach you how to INVEST. Let's look at the difference:

Definition of Investing

- To commit money or capital in order to gain a financial return

- Laying out money or capital in an enterprise with the expectation of profit

- To grant someone control by furnishing them with power or authority

Definition of Gambling

- To bet on an uncertain outcome

- To play a game of chance for stakes

- To engage in reckless or hazardous behavior

Starting to see the difference? When you gamble, you send your money to an unknown future. "Reckless or hazardous behavior" is NOT how you want to spend your Hard-Earned Money, is it? On the other hand, investing directs capital toward an enterprise wherein you are ***expecting a profit***.

The way that you can invest and expect a profit is by having control over your information, understanding the risks involved, and then confidently sending your money toward an expected financial return. Of course, no one can predict the future. If anyone knew exactly when a stock was going to go up or down in value, they would be wealthy immediately. Let's look at the actual track record of stock market returns

The Stock Market's historical rate of return

- The annual rate of return of the entire U.S. Stock Market:

  - 11% from 1926 to 1999

  - 18% from 1990 to 1999

- The annual rate of return from the stocks in the Dow Jones Industrial Average index:

  - 13.5% from 1970 to 1999

  - 18.4% from 1990 to 1999

  - 27.0% from 1995 to 1999

- Let's say that in 1802, when America was just a few years old, you invested $4 as follows:

  - $1 in stocks

  - $1 in bonds

  - $1 in Treasury bills

  - $1 in gold

By the end of the 20th century, your investments would have grown to the following amounts:

  - $1,250,000 in stocks

  - $6,920 in bonds

  - $2,830 in Treasury bills

  - $14.20 in gold (yes, only fourteen dollars and twenty cents)

Over the last 200 years, stocks have absolutely given you the best return on your money over every other kind of investment. This rock solid track record can give you the confidence that you are not "betting on an uncertain outcome." By purchasing and selling stocks, you are allowing the companies behind the stocks to have operating capital and liquidity of funds. Furthermore, the impressive returns stated above are the averages of thousands of different stocks. You are going to learn how to search for and invest in only stocks that are excellent performers. As you begin accessing information about the stock market, you will quickly come across the phrase:

"Historical performance is no guarantee of future performance."

This is a true and sobering statement. Very few things in this life are guaranteed. However, you WILL learn how to collect information that shows trends and directions of individual stocks. You WILL be making an informed investment based on data and analysis. You WILL be expecting to make a profit!

Gambling, on the other hand, is where people throw their money at an unknown opportunity hoping to gain a quick return. Let's look at two different scenarios to show the difference between gambling and investing. All of the concepts and terminology used in these scenarios are explained in easy-to-understand language in the chapters that follow.

Scenario 1

The guy in the cubicle next to you says, "Hey, I heard the value of XYZ stock is going to triple this week because of a merger." You run over to your computer, log on to your Online Broker's website, and buy $10,000 of XYZ. You just gambled!

Scenario 2

The guy in the cubicle next to you says, "Hey, I heard the value of XYZ stock is going to triple this week because of a merger." OK. Fine. **Maybe** there's an opportunity here. You use the process defined in this book to research the company that issues XYZ stock. You review the company's historical value change. You enter XYZ into a Watch List. You find out what products they sell. You think. You study. You analyze. And then, **if** you feel confident about the future of XYZ, you choose to purchase a calculated amount of their stock.

At the same time you buy their stock, you put a stop sell in place to protect your investment. In other words, before you send any money toward XYZ stock, you have a very good idea what to expect in terms of the stock's value. You will also know, to the penny, how much money you could lose if The Worst-Case Scenario happened. Now **that,** is an **investment!**

What about how risky the stock market is?

It's true, there is definitely risk associated with investing in the stock market. But remember, there is risk associated with every part of daily living. Everyday risks that you routinely take include:

- Driving to work every morning. Your car could shut down unexpectedly and leave you stranded by the side of the road. And don't forget that the statistical odds are very high that you will have a traffic accident.

- Booking a vacation. The flight could be delayed, or a hurricane could blow into the tropical paradise where you're scheduled to stay and strand you for days.

- Getting a mortgage. When you're buying a house and waiting to lock in the mortgage interest rate, the rate could jump up or down before you sign the contract.

Risk is unavoidable

Just as you can't eliminate risk from everyday living, you can't eliminate risk from stock market investing. What you can do, is work and study so that you know ahead of time what the risks are. Once you know what they are, you can take steps to minimize them.

Once you identify the risks and take all the steps you can to avoid them, it is exhilarating to be in the game. Sometimes the result of the risks you take will be small losses. Other times, the reward of taking those risks will be large profits.

I Do Not Choose to Be a Common Man

It is my right to be uncommon – if I can.
I seek opportunity – not security.
I do not wish to be a kept citizen,
humbled and dulled by having the state look after me.
I want to take the calculated risk;
to dream and to build, to fail and to succeed.
It is my heritage to stand erect, proud and unafraid;
to think and act for myself, enjoy the benefit of my creations
and to face the world boldly and say,
This I Have Done!

Dean Alfange

Summary

- If you blindly put your money into a stock without knowing how the company has done historically or may do in the future, you are gambling.

- Over the 200 plus years of America's history, the stock market has proven to be the best investment, soundly beating out bonds, Treasury bills, and gold.

- This book will show you how to NOT gamble your money by teaching you to:

  ➢ Find stocks that have done well historically

  ➢ Find stocks that have an excellent chance of doing well in the future

  ➢ Calculate exactly how much of your money would be at risk if The Worst-Case Scenario happens

  ➢ Protect your principal against drastic market downturns.

- There is risk associated with stock market investing. This book will show you how to calculate exactly what those risks are and how to minimize them.

3

Do I Have Time to Do My Own Investing?

**We've all seen them...
often in the movies or on TV...
maybe in real life...**

The "Freaks-Out-in-the-Middle-of-Life" Investor

You pass him on the street. His hair is disheveled. He's talking in a loud panic while trying to hold a never-designed-to-be-held-with-your-shoulder cell phone on his shoulder while he madly punches the stylus on a Personal Digital Assistant. "Holy monkey! The stock price of Bob's Buggy Whips Incorporated is dropping like turkeys thrown out of a helicopter!!! Sell! Sell!! SELL!!!"

The "Micro-Managing Day Trader"

He's 38, never been on a date, and spends the day in his mother's dark cluttered basement surrounded by a mish-mash of computer screens and old pizza boxes. The eerie, dull-green glow of the computer monitor reflects in the half-inch thick glass of his black horn-rimmed spectacles as his eyes dart around the screen.

"Alriiight! Atomic Pocket Protectors is finally shooting up in price! Nine dollars and thirteen cents! Nine dollars and fifteen cents! I'm betting my whole portfolio on this beauty!"

His fingers dance across the keyboard, executing a transaction and buying shares of Atomic Pocket Protectors that consumes his life savings.

"OK, baby, now, let's go through the roof! Up, Up, Up! YES! Nine dollars and eighteen cents! Yahoo! I just made a thousand dollars! I'm gonna be rich! RICH, I tell ya!"

"Huh, what's that?!"

"Down to nine dollars and fourteen cents!? OK, just a minor market correction. Only a few thousand dollars lost. No problem. Aaaaaaagh! Eight dollars and 97 cents! Oh my gosh! I'm tanking! I'm getting out while I can."

As we slowly back away from our nerd friend, we can hear the frantic clatter of the keys as he dumps Atomic Pocket Protectors and most of his net worth.

What you WON'T be

Well, Dear Future Stock Market Investor, the good news is that while these and many other neurotic stock traders do indeed exist, a much better fate awaits you!

- You are going to learn how to be calm no matter what the market is doing.

- You won't ever have to run to the phone, call your stockbroker, and scream, "Sell, sell, sell!"

- You won't have to watch the computer screen and worry about every tick up and down of a stock's price.

You WILL be able to keep your Day Job and have all the time you want for family, friends, recreation, travel, or whatever floats your boat.

Welcome to your New Part-Time Job

One of the reasons you probably picked up this book is because you're interested in earning more money than what you currently have, right? Well, there are lots of ways to bring in additional income. To supplement your Day Job income, you could take the midnight shift at Crabby's Convenience Store on the corner. That is good honest work and for trading some hours of your life, you would receive a paycheck. If you worked four hours a day, five days a week at $7 per hour, you would gross $140 a week (4 hours/day x 5 days/week x $7/hr = $140). After taxes, you would bring home about a hundred bucks a week.

To earn that $100 a week, you would have to live on much less sleep and be away from your family and comfy home. If you are one of the tens of thousands of hard-working individuals who

DO work at the convenience store, I mean no disrespect. I am merely using this as an example and am very grateful that you ARE there at two in the morning when I need Twinkies and a Slurpee.

But let's consider an alternative. What if you took those 20 hours a week that you're working at Crabby's Convenience Store and used them to make money in a different way? First of all, take 10 of those hours and, for goodness sake, get some sleep! Then take the other 10 hours and spend those on your New Part-Time Job...Stock Market Investing. You'll research stocks that will earn handsome returns, learn about the stock market, and become a Student of Commerce! Someone once said,

"If you will spend an hour a day studying any subject, then in a year, you will be an expert."

While this alone may sound invigorating, consider the additional perks of your new job:

- You can do it from the comfort and safety of your home.

- You can do your research 24 hours a day via the Internet.

- You define the dress code. If you work best in your Batman jammies, then Hey! You're the boss here, so you decide!

What kind of paycheck are we talking about?

Most people would say that an annual return of 10% is a good rate, and I would agree. If your investments all got 10% a year every year, by most standards you would be doing very well. But what if you could get 20% or 30% or 40% per year? That would be even better, right? We're going to shoot for something in that range. Sometimes you'll come in under that, and sometimes the market will reward you with returns even greater than that.

How much would I have to earn in the stock market to make $100 a week?

To replace the $100 per week take-home pay from Crabby's Convenience Store, you will need to earn $560 a month before taxes. Multiplying $560 per month times 12 months is $6,600 per year. To replace this $6,600 a year from a part-time job, you would have to invest a certain amount of money in stocks. Those stocks would then have to increase in value a certain amount. This increase in value would be your **return** on your investment. **Figure 3-1 Principal amount and return required to earn $6,600 per year** shows different combinations of amounts you could invest and returns you would have to make in order to earn $6,600 per year.

Figure 3-1 Principal Amount and Return Required to Earn $6,600 per Year

To earn $6,600 a year	
You must invest:	**And get an annual return of:**
$ 10,000	67%
$ 15,000	45%
$ 20,000	34%
$ 25,000	27%
$ 30,000	22%
$ 35,000	19%
$ 40,000	17%
$ 45,000	15%
$ 50,000	13%
$ 55,000	12%

Examples of how to use the above table:

- IF I want to make $6,600 per year, and

- I have $30,000 to invest, then

- I need to earn an average of 22% on my investments.

Here's another way of looking at the table:

- IF I want to make $6,600 per year, and

- I earn an average of 15% on my investments, then

- I need to have $45,000 to invest.

These numbers are presented just to give you a perspective on how investing can be used to provide alternatives to how you use your time and money. You certainly don't have to have $45,000 to get started. In fact, in Chapter 6, "What type of account do I want to open?" you will find ways to get started investing with just a few hundred dollars.

Figure 3-1 shows a **reasonable** range of returns you could obtain through your investing activities. You can earn 5% on your money with static investments such as bank certificates of deposit and annuities. However, the best returns are in the stock market where you are currently educating yourself as a Student of Commerce. Returns of 20% to 40% are not unusual and are certainly within your ability to capture.

If you walk into a financial planner in a glass-front office next to your supermarket and say, "Hey, what do you have that will earn me 20% to 40% returns?" you're going to have a very short conversation. You'll probably get a free lecture about how risky the stock market is and how instead, you should consider one of their nice safe investments that returns 3% to 5%. There is nothing wrong with that, and there is definitely a place for those types of investments. But what **you** are learning by studying this book is how to be a Student of Commerce who understands the risks involved, makes plans to minimize those risks and, as a result, receives **excellent** returns!

Back to, *"Do I have time to do my own investing?"* As you can see, the more successful you are at investing, the higher return you will receive. The higher return you receive, the more income you produce from your principal investment. The more income you produce, the quicker you replace the paycheck from Crabby's Convenience Store.

But don't misunderstand me...this is work, and you'll need discipline to succeed. It's my job to explain the steps clearly so that you know exactly what to do. It will be YOUR job to approach this just like a paid position where you would learn skills, accomplish objectives, and in general, have a satisfying and enjoyable time working!

How will I actually DO my New Part-Time Job?

Here's how this can work:

- You KEEP that Day Job and continue to do your very best quality work for your employer.

- On nights and weekends, you do your research and plan your transactions.

- During the day, when the market is open, you'll execute your transactions.

With access to a computer connected to the Internet, executing your transactions will take you just a few minutes. If you're able to use a computer at work, you could easily enter your transactions during a break. However,

You always want to honor your employer's rules regarding personal use of company equipment.

Let's assume that it's OK with your boss to use the company's computer for five minutes a week for personal business or, that you have some other access to a PC.

- First of all, some weeks you will have **no** transactions to enter while the market is open. Remember, you ARE NOT going to be like the "Freaks-Out-in-the-Middle-of-Life" investor or the "Micro-Managing Day Trader."

- During the day, you may log on to your portfolio to get a quick glance at how your stocks are doing.

- If your stocks are doing well, smile, log off, and keep doing excellent work for your Day Job boss.

- If you see your stocks are doing poorly, grimace, take a deep breath, AND LOG OFF!

That's the great thing about your New Part-Time Job. All of the decisions about buying and selling will be done in the peaceful time of the evening when the market is closed. If your stocks start misbehaving, you will have issued orders for them to sell automatically – without you having to do anything!

Entering transactions during the day

Your transaction list will be very short, usually consisting of one or two Market Buy Orders and maybe one or two stop sell adjustments. These terms will be explained in excruciating detail later. These transactions can be given to your stockbroker by telephone or over the Internet. It will take you longer to log on to your Online Broker's site than it will to execute your transactions. A buy order can be entered in 10 seconds.

You will always want to enter your transactions when the market is open. The market is open from 9:30 a.m. until 4:00 p.m. EST.

The reason for this is that once you get ready to execute a transaction, you want to know what the market is doing. If the market or the stocks in which you are interested are having a wild day, you may want to modify or hold off on your transactions. For example, say you have been watching XYZ stock for a couple of weeks. After careful research, you are optimistic about its future as a profitable investment. XYZ closed yesterday at $12 after going up in price about $2 a month for the last 3 months. That's a 50% increase in 3 months. If it performed like that all year, you would triple your money in a year. If it only did HALF that well over the entire year, you would double your money.

So, before you go to bed, you decide to invest the $2,000 cash sitting in your brokerage account in XYZ the next morning. You go to work and on your lunch break, you log on to your brokerage account. When you do, you notice that the Dow Jones is DOWN 142 points. When you check on the current price of XYZ, you find that it is down to $7 from when it closed yesterday at $12. What's going on here? Was there some bad news that caused the market to drop? What about your decision to spend $2,000 on XYZ? Is now a great time to buy since it is "on sale"? Or, what if it's on a death spiral and today's drop is the beginning of it going down even more and never recovering?

Again, you cannot predict the future. But what you can know is that there are too many questions right now, and you're not as confident in spending your money as you were last night. So relax! Hold on to your cash and let the market do what it's going to do. Watch the circus from the safety of the grandstand. There's plenty of time to see how XYZ is going to perform and either buy some shares later, or pass and invest in something else.

If you had entered your transaction at night when the market was closed, you would not have seen that the stock prices were jumping all over the place. That is why you only want to enter transactions during the day when the market is open. Since you will be doing your research at night and on weekends and, since entering your transactions only takes a few minutes, you definitely DO have time to do your own investing!

Summary

- With a small amount of money, you can start investing and earning returns while gaining knowledge and learning new skills.

- With an investment of $20,000 or more and good returns, you can replace the income from a part-time job.

- If your Day Job is during the day, you will research and plan your transactions during evenings and weekends.

- You will always want to enter your transaction when the stock market is open from 9:30 a.m. EST to 4:00 p.m. EST.

- With your transactions planned ahead of time, you can use a computer to enter them in just a few minutes per week.

4
What Equipment Will I Need?

Armed with a well-performing Personal Computer (PC), a fast Internet connection, an Online Broker and some online investing tools, you're going to become an investing, wealth-building, cash-generating machine! This chapter is a step-by-step guide for explaining which computer equipment you need for using the online services described in the next chapter. If you already have a computer that is ready to work on the Internet, then you can skip to the next chapter. Let's start gathering your toys...ummm, I mean tools!

The heart of your toolkit – a smokin' PC!

In order to access your Online Broker and all of the online tools, you're going to need a Personal Computer that can communicate over the Internet. If you currently have an Internet-capable PC, you should be able to get started right away. Even older PCs usually perform adequately enough to start shopping around for the rest of your tools. However, there are at least a couple of reasons why you might want to consider purchasing a new computer to use in your investing.

How speedy is your PC?

As a cutting-edge Student of Commerce, you are going to want to work and learn quickly. A PC that makes you wait 5 seconds for the screen to change can dampen your zeal for researching the vast data out in cyber space. If you're working on an older PC, you should try doing some work on a newer PC to see if the response time is significantly different. Ask a friend who has a shiny new system, or go to your local technology store and get "hands on" with a current model. If your suspicions are correct and your current machine is pokey by today's standards, plan to get a new machine.

How easy can you get to your most important tool?

Here's another important consideration. Maybe you have a PC in the house but everyone shares it. Since accessing online tools and services is a critical part of your New Part-Time Job, it is important that you have good access to your primary tool. If you have to wait in line for the kids to finish playing games with a cyber-adolescent in China, then you should consider investing in a machine of your own. If your current PC is located in a noisy, distracting part of the house, you might also consider getting a PC to work on where you can concentrate.

New PCs are cheap

You can walk into your favorite technology store and say, "Hey, Techno Salesperson, sell me your cheapest Personal Computer." What you'll get is an entry-level machine with the latest operating system that will outperform any PC you've had at the house for two years or more. I've been monitoring entry-level prices for several years now, and they have hovered around $600. While the price has remained the same, the power and technology has been constantly increasing. For accessing online services, a new entry-level PC will do wonderfully well for you.

What about all those "options" for my new PC?

PCs have all different price tags. I put optional features in three categories:

> ➢ Definitely worth the money

> ➢ Nice features, but can be added later

> ➢ Don't need

Definitely worth the money

Following are features that will absolutely bring value to your online work. You should scrape your pennies together and try to get the items in this category.

System memory

More memory helps your entire system run faster and is usually not very expensive. This is a great place to spend a few extra bucks. Check on the cost to upgrade the system memory on any PC you buy. Then, get all you can afford.

Printer

You'll definitely want some type of printer, and there are lots of choices. If you are unfamiliar with the various printer types, visit your local technology store and have the salesperson show you the different options. Here is a quick overview of the two most popular types:

- Laser printers

You just can't beat a good laser for black-and-white images that are printed fast and inexpensively.

- All-In-Ones

If you need the services of a fax, scanner, photocopier, and color ink-jet printer, these multifunction machines are great workhorses. They're surprisingly inexpensive and take up less space than individual components. The ink-jet printers are fine for small quantities and usually print a little slower than a laser.

Nice features but can be added later

Larger and higher-resolution display screen

Here, bigger IS better! With larger screens, you can have more windows open at one time. I have two screens connected to my PC and often fill them both with different windows from my Portfolio Tracking Tool. This is one of those places where you could start with the entry-level model and then buy a more advanced model later.

Wireless keyboards and mice

These are not necessary but are very popular. Once you work with a keyboard and mouse with no wires, you'll never go back. Remember, you don't have to buy everything at once. These kinds of upgrades make great birthday and Christmas presents.

Wireless router

Without a wireless router, your PC connects to the Internet through a cable from your modem. This forces you to locate your PC close the modem. By connecting a wireless router to your

Internet connection, you can position your PC anywhere in the house regardless of where the modem is. A wireless router is really handy if:

➢ You have a notebook or portable PC.

➢ You have more than one PC in the house that needs to share the Internet connection.

➢ You want to locate a desktop PC in a place that is not close to the Internet modem.

Don't need

Faster CPU

The Central Processing Unit, or CPU, is the "brains" of your PC. For online work, a faster CPU will give you little benefit unless you're used to working on a PC that is older than two years. A faster CPU **will** benefit you when you are playing advanced games or manipulating graphic, audio, or video files. Unless you will be using your PC for one of these intense cycle-consuming applications, save your money to spend on other upgrades.

Bigger hard drives

Online tools use hardly any of your hard drive space. This is because the data and programs reside on someone else's computer. The other computers are called servers, and since you access them via the Internet, you don't have to have copies of the program on your machine. If you start working with audio or video files, they can be very large and need lots of hard drive real estate. But for the online work you'll be doing, the hard drive that comes with the entry-level PC will be entirely adequate. If you start doing work that requires more disk space, a larger hard drive can easily be added later. Start with the entry-level size hard drive and upgrade later only if you need to.

Your lifeline to unlimited knowledge – the Internet

Once you have a great PC available to work on, it is absolutely required that you have a quality Internet connection. This connection to your home will be supplied by an **Internet Service Provider**, or **ISP**. There are several ways to connect to the Internet. In general, you want a connection that is fast, simple and affordable for an individual consumer's budget. I'll take a broad sweep on this subject and divide your connection options into two categories: Dial-up and Broadband.

Dial-up Internet connection

At the turn of the century, this was how most Internet users connected to the Internet. Your PC was plugged into a telephone landline and used one of its components called a modem to **dial up** another computer. This other computer was connected to the Internet. Dial-up connections were reliable and relatively inexpensive. New connection options quickly became available and had strong advantages over dial-up connections because:

> ➤ They were faster.

> ➤ They did not require the connection process of dialing a phone number, waiting for the other computer to answer, and for the connection to be confirmed.

> ➤ The newer connections were **always on.** Whenever you turned on your computer, the Internet connection was live and active.

Dial-up connections are still available, but you should only choose this type of Internet connection if:

> ➤ It is the only connection option available in your area, or

> ➤ Your budget absolutely prohibits you from spending the extra $10 to $30 per month on the faster connection methods.

Broadband Internet connection

For our purposes, we'll define a broadband connection as synonymous with a single function: Speed! To zip around the Internet like you're going to want to do, you'll want the fastest connection that is reasonably priced. While there are new broadband connection options being designed all the time, I'll mention three that may be available for you to check out. They are:

> ➢ Cable

> ➢ Satellite

> ➢ DSL

All three are excellent choices for speedy Internet connections. What you will want to do is research all three and decide which ISP can deliver the package that is best for you. Features to consider:

- Availability in your area: Obviously, if you can't get a type of service at your house, it isn't an option. If a type of service is not currently available, ask when the service will be rolled out in your area. If it's just a few weeks away, it might be worth waiting for.

- Price: It can be a challenge to get an "apples-to-apples" comparison. There are often promotional prices for the first few months of service. That's fine, but be sure to know what you will be paying after the promotional price has expired.

- Always on: If you have a choice, you DO NOT want a connection that requires you to log on every time you're going to use the Internet. When you turn your computer on, the Internet connection should be active or, "always on."

- Speed: This will be the hardest feature to compare but go ahead and try. Most ISPs will give you two speeds on which they rate their service:

> ➢ Upload speed

> ➢ Download speed

Ask each ISP how they rate their speed and what the guaranteed minimum speeds are.

- Bundled services
The trend is for ISPs to offer other services in addition to high-speed Internet. These services can include:

➢ Telephone

➢ Television signals

➢ Cellular telephone

➢ Wireless networks to go with your Internet connection

➢ Security monitoring

➢ And on and on and on

As an educated consumer, you will have to carefully evaluate each of these bundles and determine the actual value each adds to your lifestyle. There may well be some savings by bundling these services, but make the ISP prove it to your satisfaction.

Summary

- Consider buying a new PC if you:

  - Don't have a PC

  - Have to wait in line to use the family PC

  - Have a PC is more than two years old.

- Options that are definitely worth the money:

  - More system memory

  - A printer

- Options that are nice, but can be added later:

  - Larger display screen

  - Wireless keyboards and mice

  - Wireless router

- Options you don't need:

  - Faster CPU

  - Bigger hard drive

- Types of Internet Service

  - Dial-up

  - Broadband (preferable choice)

- Internet Service Provider features to consider:

  - Availability in your area

  - Price

  - "Always on" versus having to log on

  - Speed

- Bundled services: Look for bargains by combining services that you were going to buy anyway.

5

What Online Services Will I Need?

There are two critical online service packages you will need:

- An Online Broker

- A Portfolio Tracking Tool

Why do I need an Online Broker?

As explained in Chapter 1, an Online Broker is not a person, but an online service provided by a stockbrokerage firm. This service allows your computer to communicate with their computer to execute stock transactions. Your Online Broker provides several functions required for you to buy and sell stocks. For example:

> ➢ You're going to need money in order to buy stocks. Your Online Broker holds the funds you deposit just like your brick and mortar bank does for your checking or savings account.

> ➢ Your Online Broker receives your buy and sell orders and executes them on the appropriate market for you.

> ➢ Your Online Broker also provides a multitude of support services, such as statements, tax reporting, transfer of funds between accounts, etc.

What is a Portfolio Tracking Tool?

The Portfolio Tracking Tool is a suite of power tools you will operate as a Student of Commerce. It's where all the action takes place and what you will use to:

> ➢ Shop for stocks that will make you money

> ➢ Find tons of information about a stock so you can decide if you want to spend your Hard-Earned Money to actually purchase it

> ➤ Track the performance of stocks you own so you can see how profitable you are.

Which comes first – Online Broker or Portfolio Tracking Tool?

The ideal situation is to have your favorite Portfolio Tracking Tool offered as a set of services by your Online Broker.

If you already have an Online Broker:

Your existing Online Broker is the first place you want to look for your Portfolio Tracking Tool of choice. Check to see which features and services are offered in your Online Broker's Portfolio Tracking Tool and compare them to the "Must Have" features listed below. If you think that the services they offer will work for you, then you're set! You'll be able to use the services of your Portfolio Tracking Tool within your Online Broker's website. If you DON'T think your Online Broker has an adequate suite of Portfolio Tracking Tools, you have two choices:

> ➤ Sign up with a new Online Broker who has an embedded set of Portfolio Tracking Tools you like, or

> ➤ Keep your existing Online Broker and use the Portfolio Tracking Tools on another website.

I've done it both ways and know that you can make either way work. It definitely is more convenient to have everything in one place, but the important thing is to get a set of tools you can work with and get started. You can always change services later if you want.

If you don't already have an Online Broker:

If you're starting from scratch to find an Online Broker AND a Portfolio Tracking Tool, you should definitely focus your search to find both in the same place.

How do I find a Portfolio Tracking Tool?

To search for a Portfolio Tracking Tool, log on to the Internet and go to your favorite search engine. Type in the following words to search for:

- Portfolio tracking

- Investment tracking

- Portfolio management

What features do I need in my Portfolio Tracking Tool?

From the above search combinations, you will get dozens of sites to visit. Surf around and start to get a feel for services they offer. Check to see if there are any costs involved. Many sites provide excellent tools for no cost at all. As you begin to check out the different Portfolio Tracking Tools, there are certain features you must have.

Must have: Historical charting

Figure 5-1 Sample Stock Price Graph of the 3M Company is an example of a stock price chart. This figure shows the historical price of a share of stock in the 3M Company between 1985 and 2005. The vertical, or "Y" axis, represents the dollar prices of an individual share of stock, while the horizontal, or "X" axis, represents what the price of the stock was at a certain time in history.

Figure 5-1 Sample Stock Price Graph of the 3M Company

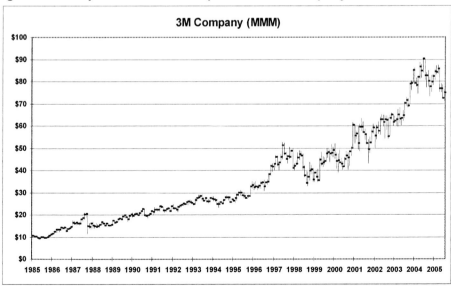

Each of the thousands of stocks in the stock market has their own unique **stock symbol**. Most stock symbols are from one to seven characters in length. The stock symbol for the 3M Company is "MMM" as shown in Figure 5-1. The charting program should let you type in any stock symbol and within a second or two, display a graph like in Figure 5-1. The charting program should also let you quickly change the timeline displayed from, say, three months to 12 months. Timeline options should also include an intraday selection where you can see how the stock's price tracks minute-by-minute on a single day. There are dozens of options with charting programs. I encourage you to experiment with at least four different ones to get a feel for the options that are available and which ones you prefer.

Must have: Watch Lists

A **Watch List** is a list of stocks that you decide you want to keep an eye on. You don't own the stocks in your Watch List, but they are displayed just like the stocks you do own. Sometimes Portfolio Tracking Tools use the terms **Watch List** and **Watch Account** interchangeably. For our purposes, we will use the term Watch List.

Must have: Multiple Accounts

Within your portfolio you will probably have:

- Multiple real brokerage accounts

- Multiple Watch Lists

- Multiple Model Accounts

For this reason, be sure to pick a Portfolio Tracking Tool that allows you to have multiple accounts. The tool should let you have as many accounts as you want. No limit is best, but at a bare minimum you should be able to set up 30 accounts.

Must have: Stock Screener

The stock-screening function gives you the ability to filter and sort stocks based on criteria you define. You will use this function to narrow down a list of stocks from the thousands that are out there so that you can take a closer look at them. Your Stock

Screener should have a healthy set of pre-packaged criteria screens that are ready to run. It should also give you the ability to create your own screens based on criteria that is of interest to you.

Not required but really-nice feature: Model Accounts

A Model Account is a special kind of Watch List and is very handy for setting up a Watch List quickly. When you set up a Model Account, you enter the symbols from your Watch List, and then specify a financial transaction to apply to each of the stocks. For instance, you can tell the Model Account to:

➤ Buy 100 shares of each stock, or

➤ Spend $10,000 on each stock, or

➤ Divide a lump sum evenly among all the stocks in your Model Account.

This is one of my favorite features of Portfolio Tracking Tools. I recommend that you choose one that allows you to set up Model Accounts.

Not required but really-nice feature: Import Transactions

As we discussed earlier, having your favorite Portfolio Tracking Tools inside of your favorite Online Brokerage account is the ideal situation. However, if the favorite Portfolio Tracking Tool you found is provided by someone other than your Online Broker, you can still have an effective and efficient suite of online power tools.

What if you are just starting your adventure as a stock market investor, but only have $500 to get going? You would need to choose one of the Online Brokers that allows you to open an account for $500 or less. There are definitely several of those out there, but their Portfolio Tracking Tool may not have all of the features you want. Therefore, you could open an account at that Online Broker and use the Portfolio Tracking Tools on another website. If you decide to go that route, there is one very important feature you want to get in your Portfolio Tracking Tool: you want the ability to **import transactions from your Online Brokerage account.**

Say you open an account with Doug's Discount Brokerage. Then also say you find a powerful online Portfolio Tracking Tool on CoolPortfolioTools.com. Look around in CoolPortfolioTools.com for a feature named something like:

"Import transactions from your broker".

When you click on that option, hopefully you'll find Doug's Discount Brokerage listed as one of the brokerages from which CoolPortfolioTools.com is set up to import data. If you see Doug's listed, you're set! CoolPortfolioTools.com will copy a set of your stock buys and sells from Doug's so that you can work with your current portfolio. If you absolutely love the Portfolio Tracking Tool in CoolPortfolioTools.com, but it doesn't offer a direct import from Doug's Discount Brokerage, you can still use it as your Portfolio Tracking Tool of choice. You will just have to enter your transactions by hand. This may or may not be a big deal, depending on how many transactions you generate. I started out using a Portfolio Tracking Tool that required me to manually enter my transactions. But since I found a Portfolio Tracking Tool that allows me to import the transactions, I'll never go back to manual.

Other great features to have

The following features are nice to have at your fingertips and are widely available from a multitude of online services.

- Company information: Here is where you can get the basics on various companies, such as what products or services they provide, where they are located, their financials, etc.

- Recent news about the company: This feature will list recent news articles that mention the company whose stock is in your Watch List. It is a place you will definitely want to study before you commit your Hard-Earned Money to a company's stock. It is also where you will go to look for good and bad news that might affect the price of stocks you own.

- Analyst ratings: Here you can see how industry "experts" are rating a stock in terms of recommended ownership. They will rate the stock with terms such as Strong Buy, Moderate Buy, Hold, Moderate Sell, Strong Sell, etc.

All of the features are tools in your hand that will enable you to make the best decision about which stocks you want to own. Each tool gives you a different type of information and each one acts as a "counselor" to you.

> *"For by wise counsel you will wage your own war, and in a multitude of counselors there is safety."*
> *Proverbs 24:6-7*

> *"Without counsel, plans go awry, but in the multitude of counselors they are established."*
> *Proverbs 15:22*

> *The Bible, New King James Version*

How do I find an Online Broker?

Just as you searched for a Portfolio Tracking Tool, the best way to find an online service such as a stockbroker is...online! Go to your favorite search engine and search for:

- online broker review

- discount online broker

There are many other related words you can search, but the two phrases above will give you dozens of choices from which to start. Just like you did while searching for your Portfolio Tracking Tool, surf on to various Online Broker websites and check out the features they offer.

What features do I want my Online Broker to have?

As has already been stated, the ideal situation is for your Online Broker to be where you get your favorite Portfolio Tracking Tool. After that, the list of features you need from an Online Broker is pretty short.

Must have: Inexpensive cost per transaction

The amount your Online Broker charges you for executing transactions is the area you will want to give the most scrutiny. You can find many Online Brokers that charge under $20 per transaction and some that charge under $7. The Online Brokers will be competing for your business. Go to each of their websites and let them do their best job of convincing you why they should be your stockbroker of choice. Some will proudly show how their fees and features compare to their competitors. This is very helpful and will give you a feel for each of the major Online Brokers.

You want to pay the very least in commission and execution fees possible. However, if one Online Broker has an amazing Portfolio Tracking Tool, yet charges a couple of bucks more per trade, it might be worth it.

Must have: NO cost to place or change a stop sell order

Stop sells will be explained in detail in later chapters. There should be no charge to place a stop sell order or to change a stop sell order. Now, once your stop sell order executes, there will be the customary fee as described in the section above. You will be placing **lots** of stop sells so be sure that the Online Broker you are considering using doesn't charge even a few cents for placing them. Most Online Brokers charge nothing for entering or changing stop sells. That's what you want.

Other services

Online Brokers are constantly adding additional services to help make you successful as an individual investor. Some of these other services are:

> ➤ Programs to track your profit and loss on transactions

> ➤ Tax-reporting help

> ➤ Statements and transaction receipts

> ➤ Advanced trading tools such as NASDAQ Level II screens Don't worry if you don't know what these advanced tools are. For right now, they're beyond the scope of what you need to know to get started.

Compile your notes

> ➤ Search the Internet until you feel like you have found the top five to ten Online Brokers.

> ➤ Carefully compare their services and fees.

Before you open an account with an Online Broker, you need to read the next two chapters. These chapters will help you answer two very important questions:

• Chapter 6: What Type Of Account Do I Want To Open?

• Chapter 7: Where Do I Get The Money To Fund My Account?

Once you have decided on the type of account(s) you want to open and how you will fund them, you will go back over your notes on the features each Online Broker offers. The type of account(s) you want to open and how you will fund it may make a difference in which Online Broker you choose. At the end of Chapter 7, I'll remind you that it will then be time to actually open your Online Broker account. For now, keep reading, Student of Commerce. You're getting smarter, and this is getting more fun!

Summary

- The ideal situation is to have your favorite Portfolio Tracking Tool offered as a set of services by your Online Broker, but you can get these two critical tools in two different online sites.

- Portfolio Tracking Tool "Must have" features:

  ➢ Historical Charting

  ➢ Watch Lists

  ➢ Stock Screener

- Portfolio Tracking Tool "not required but really-nice" features:

  ➢ Model Accounts

  ➢ Import Transactions

- Online Broker "Must have" features:

  ➢ Inexpensive cost per transaction

- Don't open an Online Broker account until you've read the next two chapters and decided on:

  ➢ The type of account(s) you want, and

  ➢ How to fund your account(s).

6

What Type of Account Do I Want to Open?

Opening an Online Brokerage account is very similar to opening a bank account. At banks, you can open regular checking, interest-paying checking, savings, and retirement accounts, just to name a few. The Online Brokers you research will also offer several different kinds of accounts. I'll mention two broad categories of accounts just to give you some idea of your choices. They are:

- Individual Retirement Accounts

- Retail Accounts

Individual Retirement Accounts

The traditional IRA and Roth IRA are two of the most common retirement accounts. You might be surprised to learn, as I was, that these accounts can be used to buy and sell individual stocks and thereby build your wealth more quickly than static investments. But first, I want to give you three very important cautions to prevent you from messing up a very structured financial instrument:

- You should not solely use the information in this book to make decisions that have tax consequences to your IRAs.

- You should definitely get the counsel of your tax professional before you make any changes to money that is in an Individual Retirement Account.

- Tax laws concerning IRAs change. What may be a rule or law when this book was printed may have changed recently. Again, check with your tax professional before making any changes to your IRAs.

Having said that, let me tell you how I got started investing. I had studied the stock market for two years before I was brave enough to make my first investment. Once I was ready to try my hand at picking my own stocks, I didn't have a lump of cash available to open an Online Brokerage account. However, I did have a traditional IRA with a few thousand dollars in it.

I counseled with a tax professional, asked the people in the IRA department of the brokerage, and did my own research online. What I found is that I could open a new IRA account with my Online Broker and then transfer the money in my existing IRA into it. I learned that if I moved this money directly from my existing IRA into my new Online Brokerage's IRA, it was called a **roll-over**, and I would have no penalty or tax consequences.

Once the money was in my new Online Brokerage IRA, I could use the money to buy and sell stocks as I chose. Admittedly, the money was now at risk of me making poor investment decisions. I was very careful with my IRA money, and after my first year, my investment had grown three or four times more than if I had left it where it was.

The good news for you is that the techniques for protecting and growing your investment are documented carefully in the book you are holding in your hand.

Important Note!

Just like with any IRA, if you pull money out of your Online Brokerage IRA, you may be subject to taxes and penalties.

Since you can't harvest the profits from the IRA with your Online Broker without possible harsh consequences of taxes and financial penalties, you might ask, "Then why would I want to bother to have an IRA-type account in my Online Brokerage account?"

- While you can't take the money out of an IRA until the qualifying age, you CAN cause the money in the IRA to grow faster by doing your own investing in individual stocks.

- The IRA account in your Online Brokerage can be a great starting place to cautiously hone your stock buying and selling skills.

- YOU are in complete control of how your money is invested. That's a very satisfying feeling.

- As will be explained in the next section, this is one of the best financial instruments on the planet for TAX-FREE profits!

Traditional vs. Roth: How is profit handled?

The short answer is, "Very differently!" There are many qualifications and requirements regarding who can contribute how much to an IRA. Following is a very general overview on how the traditional IRA works. Your tax professional will be able to advise you on exactly how it will work for you.

When you put money into a traditional IRA, you are able to deduct the amount deposited from your taxable income when you file your income taxes. This gives you a tax advantage for the year that you deposit it. For example, if you qualified to put $4,000 into a traditional IRA, you would get to deduct the $4,000 from the amount of taxable income on which your taxes are calculated.

Once you reach the qualifying age to withdraw the money from the traditional IRA account without penalty, you would pay taxes on it at that time. A possible advantage is that you may be in a lower tax bracket, so your taxes on the money may be at a lower rate than when you deposited it. An important distinction is that all of the profit your traditional IRA made is taxed when you withdraw it. Granted, it may be at a lower tax rate, but it **is** taxed.

The Roth IRA has different rules, which are much more favorable to the private investor. When you contribute to your Roth IRA, you deposit money that you have already paid taxes on. For example, if you deposited $4,000 one year, then when you filed your taxes for that year, you would not get to deduct that $4,000 from your taxable income like you would with a traditional IRA. In other words, there is no immediate tax benefit the year you contribute. You also have to be a certain age to withdraw funds from the Roth IRA without penalty. However, the powerful advantage of a Roth IRA is that when you do make a withdrawal, **you don't pay any taxes on the profit you made on your investments!**

You are reading this book and educating yourself as a Student of Commerce so that you can make money. And frankly, you're hoping to make a lot of money, right? Then the Roth IRA is a tool that every investor should have. There is no place else where your investment can double or quadruple absolutely tax free. Even if you never buy a single stock, you should open a Roth IRA and put the maximum allowable amount in it every year. And your spouse should, too!

Traditional vs. Roth: What do I want?

If you already have a Roth IRA

- Open a new Roth IRA at your Online Brokerage and follow your tax professional's directions on how to do a rollover from your current Roth into the new one.

If you don't already have a Roth IRA

- Open one at your Online Brokerage.

- Put the maximum amount allowable into it every year for yourself. If you have a spouse, open one for him or her and put the maximum allowable amount into it every year.

If you already have a traditional IRA

- Consult with a tax professional to see if it would be profitable for you to convert it to a Roth IRA. If you had a traditional IRA that was earning 4% a year and converted it to a Roth IRA that was also making 4%, it may not be profitable for you to convert. Be sure to tell your tax professional that you plan on the money in your new Roth IRA to be producing "high returns" every year for you. This information may affect his calculation and how he advises you.

- If it **is** profitable for you to convert your traditional IRA to a Roth, open a new Roth IRA at your Online Brokerage and follow your tax professional's directions on how to convert your current traditional IRA into your new Roth IRA.

- If it **is not** profitable for you to convert to a Roth IRA, open a new traditional IRA at your Online Brokerage and follow your tax professional's directions on how to roll your current traditional IRA into your new traditional IRA with your Online Broker.

If you don't already have a traditional IRA

- Unless your tax professional advises you differently, don't bother opening a traditional IRA. Put your investment dollars into a Roth IRA at your Online Broker.

The Retail Account – Where you get your spending money

The previous sections of this chapter dealt with Individual Retirement type accounts in your Online Brokerage. If you choose to move your retirement accounts into your Online Brokerage, you will have complete control over how you invest your funds for later in life. But unless you're willing to pay heavy penalties and possibly taxes for withdrawing money from those accounts before your qualified age, that money has to stay in the account. You can't pull out a couple thousand bucks for a vacation.

The next broad types of accounts we'll discuss are the "regular" investment accounts offered by your Online Broker. These are the accounts that are NOT retirement types of accounts. Some of the different names this type of account can be called are:

- ➢ A Retail Account

- ➢ An individual account

- ➢ A brokerage account

- ➢ A private investment account

For simplicity and consistency, we'll standardize on the term **Retail Account**. Here's how a Retail Account is different from an IRA or retirement type of account:

- You deposit money into a Retail Account just like you would a savings account at a bank. This is money you have already paid taxes on. Consequently, there are no tax advantages to money you deposit into a Retail Account.

- When you **buy** stocks with money in a Retail Account, there are **no** tax consequences.

- When you **sell** stocks in a Retail Account there **are** tax consequences.

  ➢ If you purchase and then sell a stock at a profit, you pay Capital Gains taxes on the profit.

  ➢ If you purchase and then sell a stock at a loss, that loss reduces the amount of Capital Gains taxes you have to pay that year.

- You can deposit as much money as you want into your Retail Account every year.

- You can withdraw as much money as you want out of your Retail Account every year. You just have to remember that you will have to pay the Capital Gains taxes on the profit you made.

What about those taxes?

Say it is February 2012, and you decide to sell a motor home you've had for a few years. You get $12,000 for the motor home and decide to deposit it in the Retail Account at your Online Brokerage. Say also that you have become an excellent Student of Commerce by studying this book and other resources. Applying these principles, you search for, research, and study stocks you would like to own. Throughout 2012, you buy and sell stocks. By December 2012, you have made $2,000 in profit on your buys and sells.

Knowing that you will have to pay Capital Gains taxes on that $2,000, you withdraw $700 from your Retail Account and put it in a regular savings account at the bank. Moving $700 might be a little more than you'll need for taxes, but you want to be sure you're covered. You're going on a ski trip in January, so you decide to withdraw $1,000 to help with vacation expenses. Since you have already put money aside to pay your Capital Gains taxes on the $2,000 profit you made, you feel fine about spending some of that profit.

The $12,000 plus balance in your Retail Account is your money to do with as you please. Just like money in a bank savings account, you could withdraw all or part of it whenever you want. Obviously, the more money you withdraw, the less you have to invest. Conversely, the more you let your profit accumulate, the more funds you have to invest.

Consider Direct Deposit

Many employers will deposit amounts from your paycheck directly into a financial institution of your choice. Check to see if your employer can Direct Deposit money from your paycheck into one of your Online Broker accounts. This is a great way to save and budget your money. Suppose that you are allowed to deposit $4,000 each year into your Roth IRA and you get paid twice a month. You could ask your employer to deposit $166.66 directly into the Roth IRA account with your Online Broker on every payday. In a year's time, you would have fully funded your Roth IRA. (24 paychecks x $166.66 per paycheck = $3,999.84) If your funds allow, you could also direct your employer to make a regular Direct Deposit to your Retail Account. This way, you are using the Hard-Earned Money from your Day Job to build personal wealth.

Summary

- As a Student of Commerce, one of your goals is increasing the overall strength of your financial health. Everyone who qualifies for an IRA should have one and deposit the maximum allowable amount each year.

- While it's true that an IRA account won't give you immediate spending money, you should still take advantage of the excellent tax break the U.S. government gives you every year. Plus, you can build your skills and wealth by buying and selling stocks in your IRA account.

- As soon as your funds allow, open a Retail Account at your Online Brokerage. Even with a small amount of principal, you can begin researching, buying, and selling stocks.

- Profit you earn from buying and selling stocks in your Retail Account is subject to the Capital Gains tax. You should set aside an amount out of your profit to pay these taxes. Consult with your tax professional on how much you should set aside and how often. A rule of thumb is that you should set aside 25% to 35% of your profit for Capital Gains taxes.

7

Where Do I Get the Money to Fund My Account?

"The evidence unmistakably indicates that you have to spend money in order to make money."

Srully Blotnick,
American Psychologist, Author

Cash!...Yeah, you gotta have some to get started

You may be thinking to yourself, "Where will I get the money to fund my brokerage account?" In a moment, we'll look at several ideas on where you can get some cash to begin investing. Before we do, let's establish a few principles about the Hard-Earned Money you would consider investing in your Online Brokerage account. The first principles we'll establish will be sources of money you do NOT want to use to fund your Online Brokerage Account.

Do NOT use money that you and your spouse are in disagreement about

If you're married, I'm sure you've discovered by now that family finances can be a delicate subject. Marriage counselors tell us that disagreements about money are the number one source of conflict in families. As you consider where to get the money to put in your brokerage account, I strongly suggest you involve your spouse in this process. There are an infinite number of issues that can bring division and conflict into a marriage. You certainly don't want your journey as a Student of Commerce to be one of them. Consider letting your spouse read this book with you, and then have an open discussion about what money you could use to open your brokerage account. You'll probably find that by working together, you'll come up with even better sources of money. In any case, you'll be in agreement, and that is extremely valuable.

Do NOT invest all of your life savings at once

One of the primary goals of this book is to teach you how to protect the original money you invest in the stock market. Another goal is to help you understand, calculate, and manage the risks associated with your investing. But be sure to recognize there is an element of risk in investing your money in the stock market. The principles in this book will help you to minimize losses and maximize profits, but unexpected results can happen.

The exception to this rule would be if it took all of your discretionary cash to make the opening deposit at your brokerage account. If your Online Broker requires a $1,000 deposit, and that is all you have, no problem! You absolutely CAN get started learning how to buy and sell stocks with a $1,000 initial investment. However, the smaller the amount of money you have working for you, the longer it will take to see results and begin harvesting significant profits. But don't let that deter you! The most important thing is to get started.

If you have between $1,000 and $20,000, consider investing half to get started. You can always add more as your experience grows.

If you have more than $20,000, I'd suggest starting with no more than $10,000. You are going to make a few mistakes so with less money, the mistakes sting less.

Do NOT invest "Mission-Critical" money

If you have money set aside for specific expenses or life events, I do not recommend putting those funds into your brokerage account at first. Again, unexpected circumstances can happen, and you don't `want to endanger the kids' college fund or your income tax reserve. You might say, "Hey, the kids aren't going to college for eight years. If I invest it in the stock market now, it will grow much quicker!" That may well be true. I'm just saying, don't risk mission-critical money like a college savings at first. When your skill as a Student of Commerce increases, you may reorganize many of your family's financial assets. Start slowly, carefully, and conservatively, OK?

Do NOT invest money you are emotionally attached to

Great Aunt Sally had a hard life. Her husband died right after she gave birth to their fifth child. As a single mom, she cleaned houses in order to feed her children and was barely able to make the rent payment. Determined to help her family avoid the hardships she faced, she fought to scrape pennies together into a savings account. Upon her death, you found out that she had left each of her children, nieces, and nephews (you!) $2,400. I would consider that $2,400 to be very special money that I would want to use for a very special purpose. Personally, if I put Great Aunt Sally's money in my brokerage account, and it lost a single penny, I would be grieved. Don't set yourself up for that kind of guilt. You'll be able to find other money that doesn't have emotional strings attached.

DO consider funding your Online Brokerage account with:

Money in a bank savings account

If the money is just sitting there earning 2% or 3% and is not in one of the Do Not Fund categories above, it might be a good candidate to deposit into your brokerage account.

Funds in your IRA accounts

As we discussed in the previous section, funds in an IRA can be transferred into an IRA which you have opened in your Online Brokerage account. Carefully consider the Do NOT's listed above. Give particular thought to the "All of your life savings at once" principle and the "Money you're in disagreement with your spouse about" principle.

Just enough to open an account

Some Online Brokerages will open your account with your first deposit regardless of how small it is. Others require a minimum opening deposit of $500, $1,000, $2,000, or more. If your discretionary funds are low, go ahead and open your Online Brokerage account with whatever you have, even if it is just a few hundred dollars. You can add to your account as often as you like, just like a bank savings account. As was discussed in Chapter 6, "What Type Of Account Do I Want To Open?", many employers can make a direct deposit into your Online Brokerage account. You might want to designate $50 a week from your paycheck to deposit in your brokerage account. This is a great way to get started and build financial discipline.

Birthday and gift cash

This is money people give you to do with as you want. If they ever ask what you did with their gift, look them in the eye and with confident excitement say, "I bought part of an emerging bio-technology company that is making products to remove the scourge of tennis elbow from our society!" They will, no doubt, be impressed.

Financial assets you convert to cash

Do you have a $1,000 Certificate of Deposit that's been kicking around for several years? You might consider cashing it in and depositing the funds in your brokerage account. Do an audit of all the financial assets you have. You might be surprised at what you have that you haven't thought about for a while. If it can be converted to cash, you have the opportunity to put that money to work for you earning great returns. Places to look for hidden buckets of cash:

➤ Stocks and bonds given as gifts

➤ Whole Life insurance policies
   Consider cashing in the Whole Life policy and replacing the coverage with an inexpensive term life policy. Consult with your tax professional first!

➤ Forgotten bank accounts
   Remember that $89 in the credit union you haven't used in three years? Use it!

➤ Refunds and rebates
   Every time you get a check in the mail for a tax refund, insurance policy dividend, retail purchase rebate, or any other extra income, consider depositing it in your Online Brokerage account. You'll be surprised how quickly these little "extras" add up!

Hard assets you convert to cash

Do you have a travel trailer or boat sitting in your driveway that you only use a few times a year? Maybe it's time to lighten up on some hard assets by selling them and depositing the cash into your brokerage account.

Can I finally open my Online Brokerage account?

Now that you have decided which type of account(s) you want to open (last chapter) and how you will fund them (this chapter), you are ready to make your final choice of the Online Broker who will get your business. Go back to the research notes you compiled in Chapter 5, "What Online Services Will I Need?" Review your notes and decide which Online Broker has the features and prices you like the best. Once you have chosen an Online Broker, answer the following questions as Yes or No:

➢ Have you identified which Portfolio Tracking Tool you are going to use?

➢ Have you decided which type of account(s) you want to open?

➢ Have you determined how you will fund your Online Broker account(s)?

➢ Have you decided which Online Broker you want to use?

When the answer to each of the four questions above is YES, you are ready to open your Online Brokerage account(s)! Log on to their site or call them on the phone. Give them all the info they want and send them your opening deposit. Ask them when your account will be ready to execute online transactions. Their answer should be about a week after receiving your opening deposit. Congratulations, Student of Commerce! You now have your own stock brokerage account!

Summary

- Do NOT fund your Online Brokerage account with:

  - ➢ Money that you and your spouse are in disagreement about

  - ➢ All of your life savings at once

  - ➢ "Mission-critical" money

  - ➢ Money you are emotionally attached to.

- DO consider funding your Online Brokerage account with:

  - ➢ Money in a bank savings account

  - ➢ IRA money

  - ➢ Just enough to open an account

  - ➢ Birthday and gift cash

  - ➢ Financial assets you convert to cash

  - ➢ Hard assets you convert to cash

- You are ready to open your Online Brokerage account when:

  - ➢ You have your Portfolio Tracking Tool identified

  - ➢ You know what type of account(s) you want to open

  - ➢ You know how you will fund your account(s)

  - ➢ You've chosen an Online Broker.

PART TWO

In Part Two you will learn:

- How to shop for stocks that will make you money

- How to practice buying and selling stocks with absolutely no financial risk

- How to protect your investment from drastic market down-turns and how to do it "without losing your life savings"

- How to calculate the exact amount of money you would lose if *The Worst-Case Scenario* happened!

**By the end of Part Two, you will be ready
to confidently spend REAL money to buy
REAL stocks!**

8

How Do I Pick Stocks
That Will Make Money?

*"Son, if it were that easy to make
money, everyone would be doing it."*

*George Huston Hart (1926 – 1978)
Father of Chris M. Hart, Sr.*

I wasn't pleased with my dad's comment. In my hand, I held the comic book that **promised** I would become wealthy by stuffing envelopes in my home. All I had to do was send in $49.95 for my starter kit, and in a few days, riches would be mine! I was a wide-eyed boy who was sure he had discovered a simple and sure-fire way to make lots of money. My dad, armed with 30 years of additional life experience, knew that promises of easy income for little effort were not just empty promises...they were usually scams. While I didn't appreciate my dad's analysis of the business opportunity I had "discovered," time proved that he was right on the money (pun intended).

If it was easy and took little time
to pick stocks that made quick money,
everyone would be doing it.

With however many years of life experience **you** currently have, I'm sure the above statement makes sense to you. So, is there any hope that YOU can make money in the stock market? Absolutely! But it will NOT be quick and easy. It will require you to pick up some new skills and choose to be a Student of Commerce. And the good news is, **you are well able to accomplish this!**

What do I look for?

There are hundreds of books written on how to pick stocks. There are thousands of very educated and talented people alive today who have invested decades of their lives in learning how to pick stocks. Since I am very interested in this subject, I continually read their books and experiment with their methods for choosing stocks. I love reading a book that summarizes in a few pages what it took someone a lifetime to learn. I encourage you to continually enrich your journey as a Student of Commerce by exposing yourself to this vast library of knowledge.

My job in THIS book is to teach you a practical and relatively easy way to **get started** in the stock market. As I said before, many ways of picking stocks have been derived by people who are much more experienced and educated than I am. And while I am continually studying their work and have the greatest respect for the scholarship they represent, I needed to find a method that would give me the confidence to get started. The philosophy I am about to describe is simple and has allowed me to build wealth and produce income.

Hockey Sticks

Figure 8-1 Hockey Stick

Figure 8-1 Hockey Stick is a picture of a Hockey Stick that is used in ice hockey. The **blade** of the Hockey Stick is on the lower left and is the part used to hit the puck. The **shaft** is the part that angles up and to the right. The end of the shaft is what the hockey player holds. Notice how the shaft slopes up and seems to keep going? Now, look at **Figure 8-2 Line Chart of XYZ Stock Price**, which shows how the value of fictitious stock XYZ has changed over time.

Figure 8-2 Line Chart of XYZ Stock Price

Notice how the shape of the line in the graph resembles a Hockey Stick? Stocks that have price graphs that look like a Hockey Stick are the ones you're looking for. Why? You remember studying Sir Isaac Newton in eighth grade, don't you? You'll remember that he was a famous scientist in the 17th century.

Newton's First Law of Motion:

"An object at rest tends to stay at rest, and an object in motion tends to stay in motion with the same speed and in the same direction unless acted upon by an unbalanced force."

Newton's First Law of Motion documents the action of an object in motion. Admittedly, the historical price trend of a stock is not an object. However, when you find a stock whose historical price trend makes a graph that looks like a Hockey Stick, there will be a tendency for it to continue in that direction. Here's what I did to get started in the stock market.

> ➤ I looked for stocks that had price graphs shaped like a Hockey Stick.

> ➤ I would buy stocks whose price trend was sloping up like the shaft of a Hockey Stick.

> ➤ I held on to the stocks as long as the price trend continued to slope up.

> ➤ I sold the stock when the price flattened out or turned down.

No stock's price will slope up indefinitely. That's where there is another similarity to Newton's First Law of Motion – the part which states, "...unless acted upon by an unbalanced force." There are an infinite number of "unbalanced forces" in the market place. These forces can make the handle of the Hockey Stick flatten out or worse, bend back down. In the following chapters, you'll learn how to monitor a stock's price change and how to plan when to sell it. But for now, let's learn how to find those Hockey Sticks!

How do I find Hockey Sticks?

More than 11,000 stocks are traded on the open market. If you started typing stock symbols into a charting program, you might get lucky and stumble on stocks whose recent price trends look like Hockey Sticks. More likely, you would get tired of seeing price graphs that looked like anything BUT Hockey Sticks. Plus, you'd be frustrated because you would know that there are some beautiful Hockey Sticks hiding in the thousands of stocks you didn't have the time or energy to type into the charting program.

Let's put that Portfolio Tracking Tool to work

Here's the fastest way to find some Hockey Sticks:

- Use the Stock Screener function to create a list of stocks to review.

- Use the Charting function to look at the price trends of those stocks.

- Identify the stocks whose charts look like Hockey Sticks.

- Make a list of stocks you want to watch further.

Screening stocks

The Stock Screener function of your Portfolio Tracking Tool will have several pre-packaged screening criteria that you can use to create your list of stocks to watch. The screening criteria can have titles such as:

➤ New 52-Week Highs

➤ Intraday High-Volume Gainers

➤ Crossed Above 50-Day Moving Average Today

➤ This Year's Winners

➤ 500 Highest-Yielding Stocks

➤ New Highs on Double Volume

➤ Up-Trending Stocks Under $10

➤ Making New Highs on Strong Volume

Each of these screens will display a list of stocks that meet those criteria. You should be able to sort the list to prioritize data elements you are most interested in. For example, one of the columns in the list of stocks might be, "Price Increase Last 30 Days." If you sort by "Price Increase," the stocks will be reordered with the biggest price increase at the top of the list and the smallest price increase at the bottom of the list.

But again, the screeners may present you with hundreds of stocks. What you're looking for is Hockey Sticks. That means you're interested in stocks whose price has **consistently risen over the last three to nine months**.

Possible names of screens that might show Hockey Sticks

➢ 100%+ Price Change in the last 30 days

➢ High Earnings Growth over 12 Months

➢ Price Volume Explosions

➢ Steady Climbers

➢ Strong Last 30 Days

➢ Bullish for Two Days and Above 10-Day Moving Average

➢ Making New Highs on Strong Volume

Customized Screens

Some Portfolio Tracking Tools allow you to define your own criteria. When you're anxious to get started finding your first Hockey Sticks, the pre-defined screens will give you plenty to search for. Since you are a proficient Student of Commerce, your knowledge of the stock market and familiarity with your Portfolio Tracking Tool will grow quickly. Defining your own screens can be one of the most interesting and satisfying exercises you do in your research. Since Portfolio Tracking Tools can vary, the directions for setting up custom screens will differ. Here are the types of items to look for:

➢ Stocks whose price is at a 52-week high

➢ Stocks that have increased 35% over last 30 days

➢ Stocks with a Relative Strength Index (RSI) value greater than 70

➢ Stocks above their 10-day moving average

➢ Stocks with closing price greater than 93% of the 52-week high

➢ Stocks with a 50-day moving average that is up (or Bull)

➢ Stocks with a volume today greater than 100% of average volume for last six months

By studying the above criteria, you will learn to see what to look for while searching for Hockey Sticks. Experiment with different criteria to see what kind of price trends you come up with. When your criteria give you some of what you're looking for, but you'd like to narrow down the stocks on your list, look for criteria that can refine your filter. For example, say you asked your screener to show you all the stocks with the following criteria:

> ➤ Stocks above their 10-day moving average

> ➤ Closing price greater than 93% of the 52-week high

> ➤ Volume today greater than 100% of average volume for last six months

When you look at the stocks the screener presents, you'll notice that many of the stocks are priced under $5 per share. These are called "Penny Stocks" because the price is so low, it just takes "pennies" to buy them. If you'd like to see only stocks whose price is $5 or more, find where you can set the criteria to specify, "Price greater than $5." This will still give you plenty of stocks to look through, but will narrow the list down to those whose price is $5 or more.

Charting stocks

Once your screener presents you with stocks that meet the criteria you've set, you will want to start looking at those stock's price history graphs. Set the history period to either nine or 12 months. As you view each stock, look for strong Hockey Stick shapes. The longer a stock's price has been increasing, the better the chance that Sir Isaac Newton's First Law of Motion will be the case. You want to buy stocks that have been steadily increasing in value over the last three to nine months.

As you flip through graph after graph, you'll start to see some stocks that look interesting. When you find these, jot down their symbols. Continue flipping through the graphs until you have 10 to 20 stocks that look like healthy Hockey Sticks. The list of symbols you are jotting down are what you will use in Chapter 9 to build your very first Watch List.

Look at your candidates closer

Take your list of stock symbols and enter each one into your charting program again. This time, specify a different time period to review. Look at each graph and enter the widest time window possible. This may be labeled "All Data" or "Max." Observe how the stock's price has performed over the long haul. Does it have a history of tracking like a Hockey Stick and then crashing? If so, cross that stock off your list. Keep looking for stocks with consistent slopes upward for three months or longer.

Considerations that aren't tied to dollars

As you find stocks that have a healthy price trend upward, find out more about them. Use your Portfolio Tracking Tool and other online services to find out what products or services they offer. While a stock's Hockey Stick-like price trend is the first quality I look for, I also want to know what I'm investing in. If a company produces products or services that I wouldn't buy because of family or moral convictions, then I won't buy the stocks of those companies, either. This decision is, of course, all yours. When you invest in a company, you are voting with your dollars to support its success and expansion in the free market place. I feel a responsibility to only invest in companies that I believe contribute to a healthy, family-friendly society. That is my personal conviction, and you will have the opportunity to form yours as you study companies and evaluate where to invest your Hard-Earned Money.

Whittle them down

Keep looking at the stocks until you have five to 15 that you're still interested in. In the next chapter, you're going to learn how to take your list of stocks and turn it into a powerful tool. This tool will let you further qualify the candidates you will spend real money on so that you can make real profits!

"I'm a great believer in luck, and I find the harder I work, the more I have of it."

Thomas Jefferson (1743 – 1826)
One of America's Founding Fathers,
Third President of the United States,
Author of the Declaration of
Independence

Summary

- Use your Portfolio Tracking Tool's screening software to compile a list of stocks whose prices have consistently increased over the last three to 9 months.

- Use your Portfolio Tracking Tool's charting software to look for price graphs that look like Hockey Sticks. Jot down the symbols of the 10 to 20 best Hockey Sticks.

- Research the stocks on your list to see what products and services they produce. Remove ones that are against your personal convictions.

- Narrow your list down to between five and 15 stocks to watch further.

9

How Do I Buy Unlimited Stocks Without Spending a Penny?

Now, I didn't say you would MAKE any money!

The Watch List – Where you learn...for FREE!

In Chapter 5, "What Online Services Will I Need?" you learned how to choose a Portfolio Tracking Tool that lets you make Watch Lists. In Chapter 8 "How Do I Pick Stocks That Will Make Money?" you learned how to find stocks that have been increasing in value for the last three to 9 months. We call these Hockey Sticks because of the shape of their price graphs over time. As you found good Hockey Sticks, you made a list of your five to 15 favorite ones. Now you're going to use your Portfolio Tracking Tool to take those stocks and make your first Watch List. A Watch List enables you to:

- See how profitable the stocks on your Watch List **would** have been if you had bought them at some point in the past.

- Track the current performance of stocks on your Watch List.

- Further narrow your Watch List to a set of stocks you MAY spend real money on. This will be called your **Alpha Stocks List**.

What about that "without spending a penny" part?

Your Portfolio Tracking Tool doesn't know (or care) what you have really spent your money on. You can enter a transaction into your Portfolio Tracking Tool that says, "Buy 1,000 shares of Universal Widgets at $23 a share," and it will obediently log an entry that says you own those 1,000 shares. Your Portfolio Tracking Tool will not require you to show it a receipt for $23,000 proving that you purchased and paid cash for 1,000 shares of Universal Widgets. Again, it doesn't care.

Play Money

We'll use the term **Play Money** when we talk about "buying" stocks when we're not spending real money. Did you ever play the game Monopoly? To broker your transactions in that game, you are issued hundreds of dollars in Play Money. You'll do the same thing when you play like you're buying 1,000 shares of Universal Widgets stock. You will enter that transaction into your Watch List so you can see how profitable Universal Widgets would have been if you had spent real money to buy real shares of stock.

What you will do next is, take the list of stocks that you made in the last chapter and enter those stocks into your Portfolio Tracking Tool. This will be one of several Watch Lists that you will create.

Caution:

If your Portfolio Tracking Tool is part of your Online Brokerage account, <u>be sure</u> you don't buy real stocks that would cost you real money.

Depending on your Portfolio Tracking Tool, the Watch List may also be called a Watch Account, Model Account, Model Portfolio, Paper Portfolio, Dummy Portfolio, or some other name that indicates these are not stocks that you actually own, but ones you are studying because you are a Student of Commerce. For simplicity and consistency, we'll standardize on the term Watch List. Find in your Portfolio Tracking Tool where it allows you to add a Watch List.

Choose a name for your Watch List

When asked for the name of your Watch List, you'll want to pick a name that describes **what it is you're tracking**. Since Watch Lists are free and easy to set up, you'll probably have multiple ones that contain different stocks you "practice bought" at different times. Here are some examples of how you might name a Watch List.

- If:
  - ➢ You've created a list stocks that have doubled in price in the last six months, and
  - ➢ You want to play like you bought them all a year ago, and
  - ➢ It is November of 2008, then
  - ➢ You might label the Watch List:

Double in Six Months – Bought Nov. 2007.

- If:
  - ➢ You've identified a list of stocks whose price graphs all look like Hockey Sticks, and
  - ➢ You'd like to know how they would have performed if you had bought them all 12 months ago, and
  - ➢ It is July of 2010, then
  - ➢ You might label the Watch List:

Hockey Sticks – Bought July 2009.

What you name your Watch List is entirely up to you. Most Portfolio Tracking Tools allow you to change the name later, so don't worry about naming it "wrong." These are some ideas on how to organize your research so the data in your Portfolio Tracking Tool "talks" to you quickly and clearly. Other ideas for Watch List Names:

- ➢ Top Technology Stocks from April 2011
- ➢ Money Magazine's "Best Growth Stocks" from Aug. 2009
- ➢ Stocks My Brother-In-Law told me about since Feb. 2010
- ➢ Random Stocks I just feel like watching since Nov. 2012

Again, the name can be whatever you want, but should help you remember:

- ➢ What type of stocks are in the list, and
- ➢ The date when you started tracking the price.

Enter the stocks from your Watch List

Some Portfolio Tracking Tools will let you enter all your symbols in the same box, some will want you to separate them with commas or spaces, and some will want you to enter each stock individually.

Make this account a Model Portfolio

If your Portfolio Tracking Tool has a feature to "Make this account a Model Portfolio," you'll definitely want to use it. A Model Portfolio applies the same transaction to a group of stock symbols. For example, a Model Portfolio may allow you to enter all of the symbols in your Watch List, and for every one of the symbols:

➢ Buy 100 shares of each stock, or

➢ Spend $10,000 on each stock, or

➢ Divide a lump sum evenly among all the stocks in your Watch List.

All of these options can give you an interesting view into the historical and current performance of the stocks in your Watch List. My favorite choice is to "play" purchase $10,000 of each stock in a Watch List because:

● It is a large enough amount to demonstrate the effect of a stock's price change.

● It is an easy number to remember and use in every Model Portfolio so that comparisons are more straightforward.

● It is a realistic amount that I might spend on one of those stocks one day in the future.

Pick a fictitious purchase date for your Watch List stocks

You can enter any date here to give you a view of how all the stocks in your list would have changed in value during the same time period. Since your strategy for picking investments will focus on stocks that are currently performing well, most of your Watch Lists will look back between six and 18 months.

For your first Watch List, pick a date one year ago today. You can always come back and make a new Watch List with a different purchase date. As soon as you finish building your Watch List, your Portfolio Tracking Tool should populate it with current stock prices and fill in the default values. Take a few minutes to look at the data displayed. We'll talk about how to customize the data next, but for now, enjoy the fact that you're watching your potential investments in the market! Now you can call your friends and say cool things like, "Wow, did you see that Atomic Pacifiers went up $3.24 today?"

Customize your Portfolio Tracking Tool's display

Experiment with your Portfolio Tracking Tool to find out how to change what data is displayed. This feature may be listed as something like:

> ➤ Select View

> ➤ Change Fields Displayed

> ➤ Modify Portfolio View

If your Portfolio Tracking Tool has a collection of pre-packaged views, experiment with different ones to become familiar with the data displayed in each one. Your Portfolio Tracking Tool may also let you specify exactly what is displayed by choosing data elements from a list. This feature will be listed as something like:

> ➤ Customize Your View

> ➤ Choose Your Own Fields

Which fields to display

Portfolio Tracking Tools label their fields differently. Below is a generic list describing the data fields that are most important for you to monitor. If your Portfolio Tracking Tool has a different name for some of the fields listed below, you might want to pencil in on the next few pages what your Portfolio Tracking Tool calls the field. Of course, that is assuming you OWN this book. If you need to purchase your own copy so that you can mark it up with wild abandon, you can order copies at www.ChrisHart1.com, or use the order form on the back page of this book. Look around in your Portfolio Tracking Tool to choose a pre-built view, or, build a customized view that displays the following fields:

- **Symbol**
  Displays the symbol of your stock

- **Quantity**
  How many shares of the stock you own

- **Average Purchase Cost**
  This is the price of each share on the date you purchased it.

- **Market Price**
  This is the last price at which the stock was trading. If the market is closed, this will be the last price of the day, or the Closing Price. If the market is open, this will be the current price at which the stock is trading. Remember that if your Portfolio Tracking Tool displays stocks on a 20-minute delay, the Market Price is actually what it was trading for 20 minutes ago.

- **Opening Price**
  This is what the Market Price of the stock was when the stock market opened this morning.

- **Price Change Today**
  This is Market Price minus Opening Price. This tells you how much the price of your stock changed from when the market opened this morning. If a stock opened at $12.53 (Opening Price) and is currently trading for $13.63 (Market Price), the Price Change Today is UP $1.10.

- **Percentage Change Today**
  To figure this percentage, the Price Change Today is divided by Opening Price. If a stock opened today at $10 (Opening Price) and is currently trading at $13 (Market Price), it has a Price Change Today of $3. The Price Change Today of $3, divided by Opening Price of $10, is 30%, which is the Percentage Change Today.

- **Gain/Loss Today**
  This is Quantity times Price Change Today. It is the total value your investment has changed since the market opened. If the

Price Change Today is $1.10, and you own 100 shares, the Gain/Loss Today is 100 x $1.10, or $110.00.

- **Cost of Initial Purchase**

  If you used $10,000 to set up your Model Portfolio, all of your stocks in this Watch List will have a Cost of Initial Purchase of $10,000.

- **Current Market Value**

  To derive this value, multiply Quantity times Market Price.

- **Gain/Loss To Date**

  This is Current Market Value minus Cost of Initial Purchase. This shows what your gain or loss on this stock would have been if you had REALLY spent **that** $10,000 on **that** date for **that** stock.

  There are dozens of other numbers that you can display. For now, we'll keep it simple so you can learn the core indicators that tell you how your potential investments are performing. You can always come back later and experiment with different views for your data.

What exactly should I be "watching" in my Watch List?

Now that you have entered your Watch List, you have a powerful tool to evaluate stocks in which you have an interest. With just a few clicks, you can begin to see stocks that you might really want to purchase and identify ones that you are glad you DID NOT buy. We'll use the "click to sort on this column" feature to let the data begin to tell us a story.

How are my stocks doing today?

Click on the **Price Change Today** column so that the positive numbers are on top. You now have a list of stocks that are sorted according to the ones that have changed the most in stock price today.

Keep in mind that a $0.50 change on an $8 stock is just as significant as a $6 change on a $100 stock.

Click on the **Percentage Change Today** so that the positive numbers are on top. This view shows you the relative value change of each stock irregardless of each stock's price.

How much money have my stocks made to date?

This technique will let you know how much money you would have made if you had really bought that stock. Click on the **Gain/Loss To Date** column so that the positive numbers are on top. Now you have a view of the stocks that would have made you the most money if you had really purchased them. Are there some big positive numbers there? If so, congratulations! You are well on your journey to identifying profitable investments.

Now, for a more sobering view, click on the **Gain/Loss To Date** column again so that the negative numbers are on top. Are there some big negative numbers there? If there are, then take a breath of relief that you didn't REALLY buy those. If there are just a few or NO negative numbers, you can really pat yourself on the back for picking so many winners!

Keep watching to see how your stocks do over time

Creating Watch Lists gives you the ability to watch many stocks at one time. By seeing how their value increases and how their performance compares with other stocks, you will see stocks emerge as candidates that you might spend real money on. Here's how to use your Watch Lists to identify specific stocks that are going to make you money.

- Every day, log on to your Portfolio Tracking Tool and pull up your Watch List.

- Using the two techniques described above, note which stocks are doing well that day and which ones have made the most money since you bought them.

- Pull up the historical charts of the stocks that are doing well and review their history.

By "handling" these stocks every day, you'll get to know them. You'll find yourself excited to see if the little darling you found all by yourself is still doing well. You'll be a little disappointed that the jewel you thought would do so well has flattened out or sunk like a boat anchor. All these emotions are part of the process. Remember, you haven't spent any real money yet...you're a Student of Commerce, researching your new field of expertise.

After a while, you'll begin to see stocks that have more Good Days than Bad Days. You'll see stocks that have increased in value and would have made you a tidy profit if you really had purchased them. Those are the ones you're looking for!

Begin creating your Alpha Stocks List

As an adjective, Alpha means:

1) Being the highest ranked or most dominant item in a group

2) First in order of importance

Since you are now an expert at creating Watch Lists, you're going to use this free and powerful tool to prepare yourself for spending real money! Go into your Portfolio Tracking Tool and create a new Watch List called **Alpha Stocks List.** Move your favorite stocks into the Alpha Stocks List account. Some Portfolio Tracking Tools will let you copy from one list to another and some will require you to type in a new entry to represent that stock. Put between four and eight of your very favorite, most profitable stocks in this list.

Now, every day, when you log on to your Portfolio Tracking Tool, look at your Alpha Stocks List like you had really spent your money to buy those stocks. If you put the four to eight stocks that have done the best in your Model Portfolio, you will typically see a few that are having a Good Day, a few that are flat that day, and a few that are having a Bad Day.

Begin to narrow your Alpha Stocks List down to between three and six stocks that you are excited about actually purchasing. Very soon, you will be ready to spend your Hard-Earned Money on real stocks...

But not before you are an expert on the next chapter!

Remember the part about "...without losing your life savings?" Read on, faithful Student of Commerce.

Summary

- Create a Watch List to see how the stocks you have been re-searching would have performed if you had actually bought them.

- Regularly review the stocks in your Watch List to see how they perform daily and over time.

- Create an Alpha Stocks List of the stocks that have captured your interest by their performance in the Watch List.

10

How Do I Protect My Money So I Can Sleep at Night?

"Rule Number One:
Never lose money.

Rule Number Two:
Never forget Rule Number One."

Warren Buffett (1930 -)
American Investment Entrepreneur

Mr. Buffett gives some very good advice. If every investor absolutely adhered to Rule Number One, everyone who ever invested in the stock market would be rich. However, we know that isn't the case.

The way that Mr. Buffett <u>has</u>, and that you <u>will</u>, fulfill Rule Number One is by doing what you are doing... becoming a Student of Commerce.

In this chapter, you are going to learn a very simple, yet very effective, way to protect your precious Hard-Earned Money.

Define your Exit Strategy

If you pick up a book and read the last chapter first – you know from the very beginning how that story is going to turn out. Owning a stock for a period of time is also like a story – it has a beginning and an end. You are going to write the final chapter of your stock ownership story at the same time you write the opening chapter. Before you buy any stock, define the conditions under which you will sell it. Let me repeat that, because the concept is very important.

Before you buy any stock, define the conditions under which you will sell it.

For example, you will decide ahead of time that you will sell a stock if it starts **misbehaving.** A stock is considered to be misbehaving if it:

- Flattens out in price for a period of time, thereby wasting your investment dollars, or

- Drops in price so that it erodes any profit you made or threatens your original investment principal.

As you continue reading, you will learn how to specifically define the circumstances under which you will sell a stock.

Ways to sell a stock

There are more than two ways to sell a stock. To lay a simple foundation for your strategy, we will first study the **Market Order to Sell** and **Stop Sell**.

Market Order to Sell

When the stock market is open, every stock listed has a price which people are willing to pay. This price changes minute by minute, second by second. The price of any stock at any moment in time is called the **Market Price**. During a business day, the Market Price of a stock can change up or down from a few pennies to tens of dollars. A **Market Order to Sell** is an order to sell stock shares at the current Market Price. When you give your Online Broker instructions to sell 100 shares of ZAPU at market, your Online Broker will immediately put your 100 shares up for sale at the current Market Price. This transaction will be executed within a few seconds.

Stop Sell

A stop sell order is one of the primary tools you will use to protect your investment. A stop sell can also be called a Stop Market Order or other slightly different names. It is important that you know exactly which sell order you are using because they can produce vastly different results. For simplicity and consistency, we will standardize on the term "stop sell."

How a stop sell works

When the stock market is open and you place a Market Order to Sell, the transaction is executed immediately. With a stop sell order, you give your Online Broker instructions to sell shares of a stock you own **once the stock's price reaches a defined price**. This defined price is called the stop sell's **Trigger Price** or Activation Price. For consistency, we will standardize on the term Trigger Price.

Whenever the stock's price rises or falls to the Trigger Price, your order to sell the shares of stock is executed. You don't have to be logged on to your computer or even awake, for that matter! The transaction happens electronically and automatically. If the stock's price drops to the Trigger Price one hour after you set it, the order executes then. If the stock's price never drops to the Trigger Price, the order never executes. Setting a stop sell order is how you write the final chapter of your stock ownership story...first! A stop sell allows you to define your exit strategy ahead of time. This takes all of the panic out of stock ownership. Stop sells are also very simple and powerful tools for capturing the most profit as your stock's price rises.

Example of where a stop sell would have been handy

Figure 10-1 Cisco Jan. 1998 to Jan. 1999 is the actual historical data for Cisco Systems, Inc., from January 1998 to January 1999. Cisco provides equipment and solutions for supporting computer networks. The rise in Cisco's stock price toward the turn of the century is legendary and characteristic of the "dot com" boom in the late 1990s. Using Cisco's actual historical price data, let's generate a fictitious **What If** scenario.

What If #1

What If in December 1998, you asked the Stock Screener in your Portfolio Tracking Tool to show you stocks whose price had doubled in the last 12 months. Cisco would have been one of the stocks presented to you because its price went from around $10 in January 1998 to over $20 in December 1998.

If, in December 1998, you had pulled up Cisco's price graph for January 1998 to December 1998, you would have seen the graph presented in Figure 10-1. You can try this on your Portfolio Tracking Tool now, if you like. You'll see the same graph.

If you had pulled this graph up, you would probably have looked at it and said something like, "Man, that's a pretty good looking Hockey Stick! It dipped down a couple of bucks in July and August but has a strong growth momentum." You would have put Cisco in your Watch List and checked on its progress every few days or so.

After Christmas and New Year's you would have seen that Cisco was still rising in price. You decide to invest some of your Hard-Earned Money. On January 7, 1999, you invest $10,000 in Cisco and end up with 400 shares because it is trading at $25 that day.

Figure 10-1 Cisco Jan. 1998 to Jan. 1999

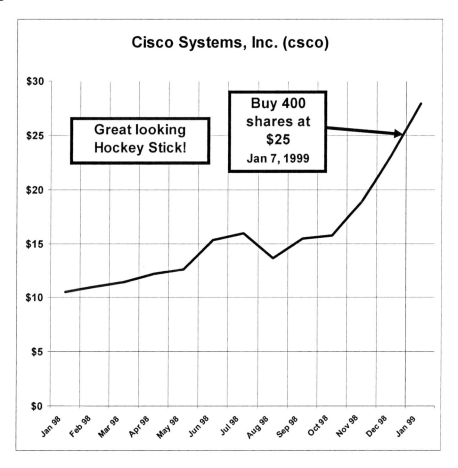

As What If #1 continues, you go through all of 1999 very happy with your purchase of Cisco. **Figure 10-2 Cisco Jan. 1998 to May 2001** shows, by the middle of 1999, the price reaches $32, and by December 1999, the price is up to $52. In March 2000, it is exhilarating every day when you log on to your Portfolio Tracking Tool and watch Cisco's stock price go from $60 to $70 and into the $80 range. On March 27, 2000, when Cisco closed at $80, your $10,000 investment would have been worth $32,000! In just 15 months, you made $22,000, or 320%.

Figure 10-2 Cisco Jan. 1998 to May 2001

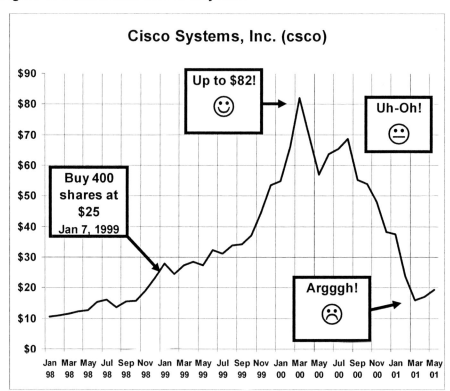

What If #1 continues...The Bubble Bursts

Late in March 2000, the stock takes a dip in price but you're not worried. Cisco has dropped $6 to $8 at other times along your journey but always bounced back to keep sloping upward.

April 2000 is a horrible month. You watch your profits erode dramatically as the price drops down into the $50s.

May 2000 gives you a little hope as the price bounces back up to the $70s, but that hope is short-lived as Cisco's price drops steadily the rest of the year.

On February 21, 2001, Cisco closes at $25.13. The $22,000 profit you had just 11 months ago is gone.

To add insult to injury, the next month, the price drops below $15. You've now lost not only the $22,000 in profit you once had in hand, but an additional $4,000 of your principal.

You say to yourself, "What a bonehead I've been! Who am I to think I could master the stock market? That financial advisor next to the tanning salon was right. Stock market investing is too risky for an individual. I should have bought that whole life insurance policy that guaranteed 3%."...and on and on and on. Before our fictitious story lets you beat yourself up too badly, check out how history could have been different...with a stop sell!

How do I avoid the tragedy of What If #1?

In What If #1, when you bought Cicso in January 1999, its price graph looked like a strong Hockey Stick. The problem is, stocks whose price graphs look like Hockey Sticks when you buy them may not go up forever. Cisco certainly didn't. In fact, a stock's price graph may end up looking like **Figure 10-3 Trajectory of a Rocket.**

Figure 10-3 Trajectory of a Rocket

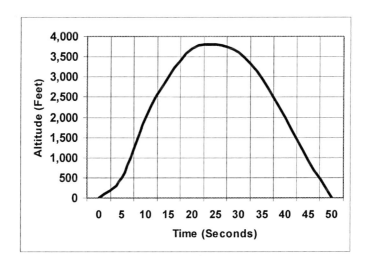

Compare Cicso's price graph in Figure 10-2 with the graph of a rocket's trajectory in Figure 10-3. Notice the disturbingly similar pattern? What you want to do is to use a stop sell on your stock to "bail out" before the price crashes to the ground. Since hindsight is perfect, you can look back at Cisco's historical graph in Figure 10-2 and confidently state that sometime after March 2000, you would consider Cisco to be misbehaving. Remember, a stock is considered to be misbehaving if:

➢ The price flattens out for a period of time, thereby wasting your investment dollars.

➢ Drops in price so that it erodes any profit you made, or threatens your original investment principal.

With these philosophy points in mind, let's look back at the Cisco graph and propose another What If.

What If #2

Refer to **Figure 10-4 Cisco from Jan. 1998 to Jan. 1999 with a Stop Sell** as you read through What If #2. **What If,** on January 7, 1999, you bought 400 shares of Cisco at $25, like you did in What If #1? In the middle of March 2000, Cisco's stock price was heading into the $70s. This made your $10,000 investment worth $28,000. While you are very pleased with your profit, you are NOT greedy and want to protect the great profit you made. **What If**, in mid-March 2000, as the stock price was going into the $70s, you set a stop sell at $65?

Figure 10-4 Cisco from Jan. 1998 to Jan. 1999 with a Stop Sell

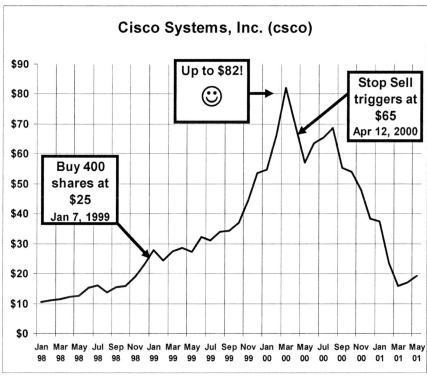

We'll talk about how to calculate stop sells in the next chapter. On March 27, 2000, you're delighted that Cisco broke into the $80s. Just a few days later, on April 12, 2000, Cisco's stock price drops to $64.75. Your stop sell triggers and sells your 400 shares at $65 each. You net $26,000. On April 14, 2000, you might be really happy you sold at $65, because the price dropped to $55. On May 1, 2000, you might be sad you sold at $65 because the price went back up to more than $71.

However, by March of 2001, you would probably be really happy again that you sold at $65, because the price had now fallen **to below $16!** The point is this:

You can never predict with certainty what a stock price is going to do. The only thing you know is what it is doing now!

This is what I base my philosophy on...What is the stock price doing now? Let's recap What If #2 in light of this philosophy.

- In January 1999, you saw that the stock price was going up so you bought it.

- In March 2000, you decided on a Trigger Price and put in an order to sell your shares of Cisco if the price ever dropped to $65 or below.

- In April 2000, when the stock price dropped to $65, your Online Broker automatically sold your shares of Cisco. You weren't involved in the transaction at all. You were busy at your Day Job concentrating on what you should have been concentrating on at the time.

The Initial Purchase Stop Sell and Floating Stop Sell

At this point you may say, "OK, I'm totally convinced I need to set a stop sell on each of the stocks I own. How do I determine what price to use when I set up a stop sell?" And THAT, my friend, is the Million Dollar Question. Anybody can buy a share of stock. Knowing when to sell it is what makes the difference between making money and losing money.

To help answer the Million Dollar Question, we're going to define two different stop sells. The first one is called the **Initial Purchase Stop Sell** and is designed to protect the original principal you invest. The second is called the **Floating Stop Sell** and will be used to capture profit as the stock's price rises. In What If #2 scenario above, there would actually have been both an Initial Purchase Stop Sell to protect the $10,000 principal AND a Floating Stop Sell in place to capture the profit of the stock's value increase. Floating Stop Sells will be covered in Part Three under the "Adjust" of the C.A.S.H. system. But for now, faithful Student of Commerce, read on to learn about the most important defense you have to protect your Hard-Earned Money...the Initial Purchase Stop Sell.

Summary

- You will never be a victim of the stock market because you will define your exit strategy BEFORE you buy a stock.

- You will pre-determine the conditions under which you will sell a stock.

- By using a stop sell order, you will give your Online Broker instructions to sell your stock if those certain conditions are met.

- You will use two types of stop sells:

  ➢ The Initial Purchase Stop Sell, and

  ➢ The Floating Stop Sell.

11

How Do I Calculate the Initial Purchase Stop Sell?

You are most vulnerable to loss immediately after you purchase a stock and before it has had time to appreciate in price. The Initial Purchase Stop Sell is designed to minimize potential loss to your principal. Notice that I **didn't** say that the Initial Purchase Stop Sell will "absolutely guarantee that you never lose a penny."

In your journey as a stock market investor, you will have some transactions that lose money. You will also have many transactions that make a handsome profit and some transactions that will make a whole wheelbarrow full of money for you! The Initial Purchase Stop Sell is where you define the maximum amount of money you want to risk losing on a transaction. Yes, that's right; YOU decide the most that you can lose. When determining where to set the Initial Purchase Stop Sell, there is a trade-off between:

➢ How much money you are willing to risk losing, and

➢ The likelihood that the stock's price will drop to the Trigger Price and execute your Initial Purchase Stop Sell.

Consider this:

- The closer your Initial Purchase Stop Sell is to your purchase price, the less money you risk losing.

- However, the closer you set the Initial Purchase Stop Sell to the purchase price, the more likely the stop sell will execute because of the stock's normal up and down price fluctuations. The corollary is also true.

- The bigger the gap between the purchase price and the Initial Purchase Stop Sell, the more money you risk losing.

- However, the bigger the gap between the purchase price and the Initial Purchase Stop Sell, the less likely the stop sell will execute because of normal price fluctuation.

What's a Student of Commerce to do? As with all ambiguous areas of life, let's set some guidelines.

Guidelines for calculating the Initial Purchase Stop Sell

Calculate a 5%, 10%, and 15% loss

Say you have $1,000 to invest in HEYU stock, and the stock price is currently $40. You want to calculate the most you are willing to lose on your purchase of HEYU. Now of course, you don't **want** to lose a single penny of your Hard-Earned Money. But there is a risk that right after you buy HEYU, the price could drop drastically.

In my personal investing, I have identified a stock which had a very well defined Hockey Stick-shaped price graph. By all indications from my research, it looked like a strong, safe investment. I then bought that stock, put it in my Initial Purchase Stop Sell, and had it plunge in price the same day, triggering my stop sell. This doesn't happen very often and certainly doesn't happen the majority of the time, but it does happen. When it does, you'll be sad for the loss, but you'll be happy that you determined ahead of time the maximum amount of principal you could lose.

Having said that, consider **Figure 11-1 Maximum Amount of Principal to Risk.** This chart shows the simple math you should do to calculate the range of loss you are willing to risk with your stock purchase. You can easily do these calculations manually. This chart is available as a spreadsheet which you can download at www.ChrisHart1.com.

Figure 11-1 Maximum Amount of Principal to Risk

| Stocks To Buy Worksheet | | | | | Maximum Amount of Principal at Risk | | | | | |
| | | | | | 5% | | 10% | | 15% | |
Stock Symbol	Current Price	Amount to Invest	Shares Will Get	Initial Purchase Stop Sell	Stop Sell	Max Loss	Stop Sell	Max Loss	Stop Sell	Max Loss
HEYU	$ 40.00	$ 1,000	25.0		$38.00	$ 50	$36.00	$ 100	$34.00	$ 150

Look at the column that shows a 10% maximum loss. This shows that if you bought HEYU at $40, set an Initial Purchase Stop Sell for $36, and it triggered, you would lose $100. You can also easily make the calculations for a 5% loss and a 15% loss.

You can experiment with different percentages of loss, stop sell prices, and max loss amounts. Doing this allows you to get a full understanding of the amount of money you are putting at risk. The next two sections will explain other criteria to consider when setting the Initial Purchase Stop Sell.

Calculate the Average Day Range

The next thing you want to look at is the price range in which a stock bounces around on a daily basis. We'll call this the **Average Day Range**. It is important to have a sense of what the Average Day Range is so that you won't set a Trigger Price too close to the active Market Price. If a stock's Average Day Range is $2, it means that according to recent history, the price will fluctuate up or down $2 from its Market Price. We will define recent history as the last three to six months. You will study a longer period of time in the next section when identifying the Biggest Price Drop.

As you know by now, anything can happen with a stock's price. You may study a stock's recent history and see that in the last six months, it has always fluctuated within a $2 band. That's all fine and good, but something drastic could happen that causes the stock's price to shoot up or down $10. There are no guarantees. Getting a sense of the Average Day Range is simply another tool you will use as a Student of Commerce.

OK, how do we figure out what a stock's Average Day Range is? Look at **Figure 11-2 Daily Trading Ranges for 3 Months**. This style of stock price chart is called a **High/Low/Close**. Each of the bars represents a week in the months of March, April, and May for the fictitious stock, HEYU.

The top of each High/Low/Close bar indicates the highest price the stock traded for during the week and the bottom of the bar the lowest price. The little tick mark sticking out of the right side of each bar is the price the stock closed at that day.

The vertical bar on the left is the Y Axis and shows the stock's price change in one-dollar increments. If it is June and you are looking at the price graph, you will see that it has a good Hockey Stick shape and may be a good candidate for your investment dollars.

In March, HEYU's price traded in the low $20s, climbed into the high $20s in April, and then on into the mid $30s in May. To get a sense of the **average** range of the stock's price trades each day, look for the shortest and then the tallest of the High/Low/Close bars.

Figure 11-2 Daily Trading Ranges for 3 Months

You can see that on many days, the range of the stock's price is a dollar or less. Many of the bars also have a $2 or $3 range. It looks like there are only two bars that are more than $3. The actual mathematical average of the daily ranges is a little over two dollars. It is always better to round up the Average Day Range, so $3 would be a good working number. Jot down $3 as your Average Day Range. Now you're ready to calculate your final criteria for setting the Initial Purchase Stop Sell: Biggest Price Drop.

Identify the Biggest Price Drop

For our next picture of this stock's performance, we will use a simple line chart. Each diamond shows the stock's price when the market closed that week. The diamonds are connected by lines to show the trend of the stock's price. When looking for the Biggest Price Drop for your stock, it is a good idea to look back from nine to 18 months. **Figure 11-3 Biggest Price Drop Over 15 Months** is a line chart of HEYU, the same stock as in Figure 11-2, but for 15 months instead of three. The boxed section on the right shows the same three months as in Figure 11-2.

Notice that by reviewing a longer period, you see that several times the stock's price dropped down by $4. With the benefit of this wider view of the stock's price trend, it would be reasonable to set the Biggest Price Drop for HEYU at $4.

Figure 11-3 Biggest Price Drop Over 15 Months

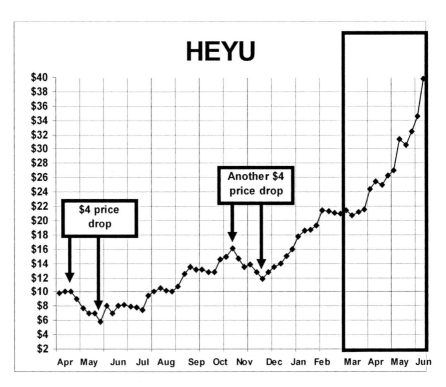

Use your data to make a decision

At this point, you have estimated that the Average Day Range is $3 and the Biggest Price Drop is $4. Now look back at Figure 11-1 and you will begin to see the importance of knowing the Average Day Range and the Biggest Price Drop. If you wanted to only risk 5% of your principal, you would have to set your Initial Purchase Stop Sell at only $2 less than the current Market Price of $40.

Since you have determined that:

➢ The Average Day Range is $3, and

➢ In the last 15 months the Biggest Price Drop of $4 has happened twice, then

➢ Chances are very good that if you set your stop sell at $2, it would be triggered by normal daily fluctuations in the current Market Price.

On the other hand, risking 10% of your principal requires you to set the Initial Purchase Stop Sell at $36, which is $4 less than the current Market Price of $40. If the stock behaves as it has in recent history, it **should** fluctuate within this $4 window and not trigger your Initial Purchase Stop Sell. If for some reason the stock's price DID drop drastically and trigger your stop sell, you would lose $100 instead of $50.

What would **I** do? Since the stock has such a strong Hockey Stick shape to it, I would tend to think it will continue to rise. Therefore, I would risk the additional $50 and set the Initial Purchase Stop Sell at $36. This would give the stock's price more room to move around without triggering my Initial Purchase Stop Sell.

What should **you** do? THAT, my friend is one of the great advantages of the Free Trade System we enjoy in America and many other countries. You have the freedom to study, learn, and make your own financial decisions. Now, let's review how you're going to make your decision.

➢ Take the current Market Price. In this example, it is $40.

> ➤ Take the LARGER of the Average Day Range and the Biggest Price Drop. In this case, the Biggest Price drop of $4 is the larger number.

> ➤ Subtract the larger number from the current Market Price ($40 - $4 = $36).

> ➤ Look at the various stop sell prices and amount of money you could lose between 5% and 15%.

> ➤ As a rule of thumb, consider setting your Initial Purchase Stop Sell between 8% and 10%. If you lose more than 10%, it will be harder to make it up on subsequent transactions. Many expert investors suggest 8%.

> ➤ Think. Pray. Determine a number.

Once you have decided on a number for the Initial Purchase Stop Sell, record it in the center column of your Stocks To Buy Worksheet (Figure 11-1).

The next chapter will walk you through deciding how many stocks to buy and how much to spend on each one. Once you have decided that, you will be able to finish filling in the Stocks To Buy Worksheet in preparation for actually purchasing the stocks.

We stated earlier that the Initial Purchase Stop Sell is your key defense against catastrophic loss of your principal. To paint a picture of how important and powerful the Initial Purchase Stop Sell is, let's go ahead and ask the question you may have been wondering about:

What is the very WORST that could happen?

As I have mentioned many times, there is a risk that your stock's price will go down after you purchase it. As you learned in the preceding paragraphs, you can determine ahead of time how much of your principal you want to risk. So that you will know exactly what you're walking into, let me lay it out for you...

The Worst-Case Scenario

Let's say you found a stock named Universal Widgets that had a great Hockey Stick-shaped price line. You open your Portfolio Tracking Tool and put Universal Widgets into your Watch List. You continue to monitor the stock's price and graduate it from your Watch List to your Alpha Stocks List. Confident about the stock's performance, you decide to go ahead and buy 100 shares of Universal Widgets at $54 per share. You spend $5,400 to buy 100 shares of Universal Widget.

After seeing that the Average Day Range is $4, you decide to risk 9%, or $500, of your $5,400 principal in order to set an Initial Purchase Stop Sell at $49. Right after you issue the order to buy 100 shares of Universal Widgets, you issue an Initial Purchase Stop Sell order to **sell** 100 shares of Universal Widgets if the price goes down to $49. You bought at $54 and have an Initial Purchase Stop Sell in place for $49.

IF your Initial Purchase Stop Sell is executed, selling the 100 shares at $49, you would be left with $4,900. So, you know going into your investment with Universal Widgets that if The Worst-Case Scenario happens, you would lose $500. Continuing our scenario, say that after you bought your 100 shares of Universal Widgets **and** placed your Initial Purchase Stop Sell at $49, you faithfully went back to work at your Day Job. **One hour** after you bought stock in Universal Widgets, all TV shows are interrupted with a Special News Bulletin:

"All across the country, the hands of people who use Universal Widgets products have turned bright blue! Furthermore, this condition seems to be irreversible! Thousands of angry blue-handed people are storming the corporate headquarters of Universal Widgets....."

That would be what the business world calls, **A Bad Day**. The stock market responds to this horrible news. The price of Universal Widgets falls from $54.68 to $32! However, then the stock's price hits $49, it triggers your stop sell and sells your 100 shares.

When you get home from your Day Job, you turn on the TV and learn about the tragedy involving Universal Widgets. Horrified, you run to your computer, log on to your Online Broker, and pull up your account. Sure enough, you see that your purchase of

Universal Widgets that you made at 10:30 a.m., sold an hour later at a loss.

You stare at the screen. You think to yourself, "Oh my gosh! I just LOST $500 of my Hard-Earned Money!" A few seconds later you realize, "I just bought High and sold Low! Some investor I am! My spouse is gonna kill me. I should've just bought that Certificate of Deposit at the bank that paid 2.13% a year, GUARANTEED!"

Hold on! Take it easy! Don't panic and don't beat yourself up. This is indeed **The Worst-Case Scenario.** Yes, you LOST $500. There is no minimizing that. But let's take a deep breath, step away from the computer screen, and benefit from perspective:

> ➢ You had a plan.

> ➢ You knew in advance the very most money you could lose on this transaction.

> ➢ You were in control. Your plan worked! Your stop sell protected you!

Even though your Universal Widgets stock sold at $49, you could have been left holding the stock at its current price of $32. In other words, if your stop sell hadn't triggered at $49, your investment would only be worth 100 shares times $32, or $3,200. So the bright side is the stop sell you created captured the stock price at $49, giving you $4,900 in real cash. That's $1,700 MORE than if your stop sell hadn't been in place and you still owned the stock. Even though a $500 loss is no fun, it could have been $1,700 worse!

So cheer up. Yes, you did have a Bad Day. But there will be other transactions that will go much better. In fact, some of your transactions will be like...**The Best-Case Scenario**.

What is the very BEST that could happen?

As in The Worst-Case Scenario, you buy 100 shares of Universal Widgets at $54. At the same time, you enter an Initial Purchase Stop Sell for $49.

When you come home from your Day Job, you have a nice dinner with the family and then decide to see how your portfolio is doing. You log on to your Portfolio Tracking Tool and see that Universal Widgets ended the day at $56.25. That's $2.25 up from what you bought it for at $54. You may be tempted at this time to move your Initial Purchase Stop Sell up to $54 so that your principal would be completely protected. Here's why that's a bad idea:

> ➤ Remember that you only enter orders when the stock market is open. Weird things can happen overnight!

> ➤ The stock's price is still within the Average Day Range of $4.

Over the next week, you're delighted to see the stock's price inch up to $59. NOW, you can move the Initial Purchase Stop sell up from $49 to $54. That's because if the stock's Market Price is $59, and it stays within the $4 Average Day Range, it will not trigger your stop sell. From here, you're home free. As long as you keep the stop sell above your purchase price, you will not lose any of your principal.

To continue The Best-Case Scenario, the price of Universal Widgets continues to rise. It becomes a very profitable stock in your portfolio, and you manage it actively using the C.A.S.H. system, which is explained in Part Three. You go to bed at night a **very** happy Student of Commerce.

How about real life?

Real life has risks and surprises. By learning the principles in this book and dedicating yourself to being a good Student of Commerce, you will have:

> ➤ Very few Worst-Case Scenarios

> ➤ A lot of good investments that give you a handsome return, and

> ➤ More Best-Case Scenarios than you may think!

Are you ready? Let's roll!

Summary

- The Initial Purchase Stop Sell is used to protect your initial principal investment from a drastic drop in a stock's price after you buy it.

- Calculate what the Initial Purchase Stop Sell would be if the stock's price dropped 5%, 10%, or 15%.

- Calculate the Average Day Range: The average amount a stock's price goes up and down on a typical day during the last three to six months.

- Calculate the Biggest Price Drop: The biggest amount a stock's price dropped over a period of weeks during the last nine to 18 months.

- Crunch the numbers:

  - ➢ Take the LARGER of the Average Day Range and the Biggest Price Drop. Subtract the larger number from the current Market Price of the stock.

  - ➢ Compare that number to the various stop sell prices and amounts you could lose between 5% and 15%.

- Use your best Student of Commerce analysis on the data before you. Decide on a number for your Initial Purchase Stop Sell. Write that number down and draw a circle around it.

- Once you know what the Worst-Case Scenario is, you can invest confidently and without fear of some unknown disaster.

- The principles in this book will be the tools you need to produce The Best-Case Scenario over and over again!

12

How Do I Spend Real Money to Make Real Money?

OK, by now you have:

- Learned how to shop for stocks that will make you money

- Set up a Watch List to see how the stocks on your Watch List would have performed

- Learned how to protect your investment from market downturns by using stop sells

- Learned how to calculate your Initial Purchase Stop Sell to protect your investment principal.

It's time to do the Real Deal.

Plan every detail of your stock purchase

Before you log on to your Online Broker to execute your stock purchase, you want to be completely prepared. Go through each of the planning steps below and **write down** the different components of your transaction.

Plan how much to spend on your stock purchase

In Chapter 7, "Where Do I Get The Money To Fund My Account?", we talked about how to fund your Online Brokerage account. In order to purchase your stocks, you need to now have those funds deposited and available as a cash balance. You should be able to log on to your Online Brokerage account and see the cash balance that you are going to use to buy stocks with. If you're not sure how to do this, you can call a customer service rep at your brokerage. Ask him to tell you where to look within online account to see the amount of your cash balance.

Now, how much to spend? Well, part of that equation depends on how much you have available to spend. In general, you want to be conservative at first while you are getting to know how to use your Online Brokerage tool. Here are some guidelines:

> ➢ If you have $1,000, consider spending $500 on two different stocks.

> ➢ If you have $3,000, consider spending $1,000 on three different stocks.

> ➢ If you have $5,000, consider spending $1,000 on five different stocks.

If you have more than $5,000, I would still only buy $1,000 worth of five different stocks. Leave the rest of the money in your brokerage account for now. You can come back any time and spend any amount of your Hard-Earned Money any way you want. But if this is your first stock purchase, I'd recommend spending a modest amount until you're more familiar with how the market and your Online Broker work.

Plan how many different stocks to buy

As stated in the above recommendations, you should buy at least two different stocks, but no more than five. You don't want to spend all your money on one stock because then all of your hopes will be tied to a single company. You want at least two different stocks in your portfolio because every stock has its up and down days.

I don't recommend owning more than five when you are starting. You want to continue being a Student of Commerce who watches, researches, and learns about the different stocks that are of interest to you. If you own any more than five, your attention may be too divided.

Plan which stocks to buy

OK, it's time to decide which stocks will be purchased with your Hard-Earned Money. This shouldn't be a very difficult task, because you have been finding stocks of interest to you, putting them in a Watch List, and watching them. You then pulled the ones you really liked into your Alpha Stocks List. This is where you will go to find the ones you will buy.

Look over your Alpha Stocks List one last time. See which stocks in your Model Portfolio have made the most money. Pull up their charts and review how they have done in the last year. Pick the two, three, four, or five stocks that are your very favorites. Those are the ones that are going into your final list:

The Stocks To Buy Worksheet

Look at **Figure 12-1 Stocks To Buy Worksheet**. You'll notice that this is the same spreadsheet we used in Figure 11-1 to calculate the maximum amount of principal at risk in setting up an Initial Purchase Stop Sell. You can easily do these same calculations with a pen, pad of paper, and calculator. If you are at all handy at making spreadsheets, you can create this same spreadsheet in a few minutes. Or, you can go to www.ChrisHart1.com and download one that's ready to use.

Figure 12-1 Stocks To Buy Worksheet

Stocks To Buy Worksheet				Initial Purchase Stop Sell	Maximum Amount of Principal at Risk					
					5%		10%		15%	
Stock Symbol	Current Price	Amount to Invest	Shares Will Get		Stop Sell	Max Loss	Stop Sell	Max Loss	Stop Sell	Max Loss
HEYU	$ 40.00	$ 1,000	25.0		$38.00	$ 50	$36.00	$ 100	$34.00	$ 150
YME	$ 62.40	$ 1,000	16.0		$59.28	$ 50	$56.16	$ 100	$53.04	$ 150
OHNO	$ 18.10	$ 1,000	55.2		$17.20	$ 50	$16.29	$ 100	$15.39	$ 150

Let's say you have $3,000 in your Online Brokerage account that you'd like to invest. As recommended above, you're going to buy $1,000 worth of three different stocks. You've looked over your Alpha Stocks List and decided that you want to buy shares of HEYU, YME and OHNO.

- In the column labeled, Stock Symbol, enter the three stocks you've chosen.

- Using your Portfolio Tracking Tool, look up the current Market Price of HEYU, YME, and OHNO. Enter that price in the Current Price column.

- Since you decided to spend $1,000 on each of the three stocks, enter that amount in the Amount to Invest column.

- For each of the stocks, divide the Amount to Invest by Current Price. This will tell you how many shares you will get for that amount of money. In the case of HEYU, you divide $1,000 (Amount to Invest) by $40.00 (Current Price) to get 25.0 shares. Enter 25.0 in the Shares Will Get column.

Important Note!

Even while you are taking these few minutes to do your calculations, the Market Price of your stock is changing.

You'll want to check the Market Price again right before you hit the Enter key to execute your buy.

- For each of the stocks, calculate the Maximum Amount of Principal at Risk for 5%, 10%, and 15% losses. Fill in the amounts under the appropriate columns.

- Using the technique you learned in the last chapter, use your Portfolio Tracking Tool to look at historical price lines for each of the stocks. Decide what the Average Day Range and Biggest Price Drop are for each of the stocks. Using all of this data, calculate the Initial Purchase Stop Sell for each of the stocks on your Stocks To Buy Worksheet. In the center column, fill in the amount you want to use for the Initial Purchase Stop Sell.

- At this point, you should have all of the columns of your Stocks To Buy Worksheet filled in for each of the stocks you plan to buy.

"October. This is one of the peculiarly dangerous months to speculate in stocks. The others are July, January, September, April, November, May, March, June, December, August, and February."

Mark Twain (1835-1910)
American Humorist, Writer

The best time to buy

Buy your stocks: When the market is open

Since you are going to be placing a Market Order, you only want to execute your buy order when the stock market is open. In general, you want the stock market to be having a fairly "normal" day. You also don't want the stock you are buying to be nose-diving! The only way to get a sense of these conditions is by looking at a live, minute-to-minute market. Don't enter your Market Order at night when the market is closed. Weird things can happen in the night!

Buy your stocks: In the morning

This is by no means a hard and fast rule, but a general principle I prefer. In general, when the market first opens at 9:30 a.m. EST, prices on stocks can shoot up and down wildly. By around 10 a.m. EST, things have pretty well evened out and the market is going to go in the general direction that it wants to that day. If you have a choice, wait until after 10:00 a.m. EST to place your Market Order.

Buy your stocks: When the stock's price is increasing

As I've said before, countless people have derived calculations to predict when a stock's price is going to increase. Some of these calculations work some of the time. But to get yourself started, you searched for Hockey Sticks that have had a steadily increasing price for the last three to nine months. For now, you're going to trust Sir Isaac Newton's First Law of Motion and believe that the stocks on your Stocks To Buy Worksheet will "...tend to stay in motion with the same speed and in the same direction." If you see that the stock's price has flattened out or dropped in a way that is uncharacteristic to its previous Hockey Stick shape, you might want to pass on buying it now.

Buy your stocks: After its price passes its former all-time high

Let's say that stock YME is in your Alpha Stocks List and has had a strong Hockey Stick price trend for several months. Then say that YME reached an all time high of $42. After reaching $42, YME dipped down to $40.50 and hung around there for four days. On the fifth day, YME took back off and went to $41, $41.50, and on up to $42.28. Once you saw that YME had passed its former all time high of $42, it would be a good time to buy. Often, when a stock "breaks through" its former all time high, it will continue to climb for length of time. This strong period of growth is a great time to bump your Floating Stop Sell up so that you get past the Purchase Price as quickly as possible. Floating Stop Sells are discussed in detail in Chapter 15, titled "Adjust."

Review each stock's price one last time

Use your Portfolio Tracking Tool to check the prices of each stock on your Stocks To Buy Worksheet. If a stock's price has changed significantly, you may need to re-do the math for the Shares Will Get column and your Initial Purchase Stop Sell. You may also want to reconsider if you still want to purchase it today.

Ready? OK, let's do it!

Execute your first stock purchase

Log on to your Online Broker. Navigate to the area in your Online Broker where you enter orders. This may be called:

- ➤ Trade Stocks
- ➤ Order Entry
- ➤ Buy and Sell Equities, or
- ➤ Something else

The Order Entry screen of your Online Brokerage account will have fields for you to fill. The fields may be named slightly differently from broker to broker. Following is a list of the fields you will need to fill in so that you can execute your transaction. You will refer to your Stocks To Buy Worksheet for the actual values.

- **Action:**
  Select **Buy.**

- **Quantity:**
  Enter the number from the **Shares Will Get** column on your Stocks To Buy Worksheet. Round **down** the number of stocks to the next whole number so you don't spend more cash than you planned or have.

- **Symbol:**
  Enter the stock's symbol here.

- **Order type**
  This is very important, because there are multiple types of Buy orders. Be sure you select **Market Order.**

- **Expiration Date**
  Select "Day" or whatever term your broker uses to indicate that you want to buy this stock **now**. Do not enter a date in the future. Do not enter "Market on Close." Market on Close means that your order will be executed when the market closes for the day, which might be hours from now.

- **Other fields**
  The above fields should be adequate to execute your stock purchase. Your Online Broker will probably have additional fields where you can modify the transaction. The default values in these other fields should be adequate to make a straightforward Market Order.

Click on the button that executes the transaction. Your Online Broker may present a summary of the order for you to review. Carefully check to be sure you entered the data correctly. If you didn't, go back and change the order, resubmit it, and check it again. Once you've checked the transaction, click the appropriate button to place the order.

Now, before you do anything else, you have got to enter your Initial Purchase Stop Sell. Do not take a bio-break or a nap. Do not get a bite to eat or go pick up the kids. It's important to enter your Initial Purchase Stop Sell right now to protect yourself against The Worst-Case Scenario.

Execute your Initial Purchase Stop Sell

Navigate back to the area of your Online Broker where you enter orders. To enter your Initial Purchase Stop Sell, you're going to fill in the same fields but with different information.

- **Action:**
  This time, select **Sell.**

- **Quantity:**
  Enter the exact number of shares you entered for the **Buy** transaction of this stock.

- **Symbol:**
  Enter the same stock symbol as you did for the Buy.

- **Order type**: You want to specify a **stop sell** order. Your Online Broker may call this a Stop Market Order or some other similar term. DO NOT enter Market Order, Limit Order, or Stop Limit.

- **Trigger Price**
  This may also be called Activation Price or something similar. Here is where you enter the dollar amount of the Initial Purchase Stop Sell that you so carefully calculated.

- **Expiration Date**
  You want this stop sell active and in place until **you** change it. Do not choose the option, "Day." If you did, when the market closed, your stop sell would be canceled at the end of the day. Choose **GTC**, which stands for **Good Til Canceled.** With some Online Brokers, GTC means that the stop sell will stay in effect indefinitely. That is what you want. **Warning!** Some Online Brokers will accept GTC as an expiration of your stop sell but will still cancel the stop sell in 30, 60, or maybe 90 days after you place it. You need to find out if your Online Broker automatically cancels your stop sell when you specify GTC for the Expiration Date. If they do, you will have to come back to your stop sell before the

Expiration Date and push the Expiration Date into the future. This is usually not a problem, because you will be updating your stop sells anyway. Once you've reviewed the details of your Initial Purchase Stop Sell, click the button to execute the transaction.

Check to be sure your orders were executed correctly

You will now be able to go to the area in your Online Broker where your stock purchases are listed and see YOUR stock symbol listed along with the corresponding quantity of shares you purchased. If you don't see what you think you should, try and figure out what went wrong. You might need to call the Online Broker's customer service line.

Now go to the area of your Online Broker where you can display pending orders. Here you should see the Initial Purchase Stop Sell you entered. Check to make sure that the Quantity, Order Type, Trigger Price, and Expiration Date are all correct. If they are not, you should be able to cancel or edit that order and re-enter the correct information.

Enter the rest of your stock purchase orders

Continue issuing Market Orders to buy the rest of the stocks listed on your Stocks To Buy Worksheet, along with their corresponding Initial Purchase Stop Sell orders. Once you've done this for the two to five stocks on your Stocks To Buy Worksheet, you will have created your first stock portfolio!

Watch your portfolio's value change before your eyes

As soon as you have executed your stock purchases, your Online Broker will start updating the stocks' prices. Immediately, the numbers for your stocks will start to change in real-time. In the chapters that follow, you will learn a powerful technique for managing, protecting, and growing your portfolio.

Summary

- Plan how much to spend on your stock purchase.

- Plan how many different stocks to buy.

  ➤ Start with at least two

  ➤ No more than five

- Plan which stocks to buy.

  ➤ Fill in your Stocks To Buy Worksheet with your favorite stocks listed on your Alpha Stocks List.

- Plan when to make your stock purchase.

  ➤ When the market is open

  ➤ In the morning

  ➤ When the stock's price is increasing

  ➤ After its price passes its former all-time high

- Review the stock's prices right before you enter the Market Order.

- Execute your stock purchase.

- Execute your Initial Purchase Stop Sell.

- Check to be sure your orders were executed correctly.

- Repeat the process until you have purchased the two to five stocks on your Stocks To Buy Worksheet AND entered the corresponding Initial Purchase Stop Sells.

- Display your portfolio so that you can enjoy watching the value of your investments change as the market does!

PART THREE

In Part Three you will learn:

- What to do now that you are an official Stock Market Investor

- How to watch and manage your investments using the C.A.S.H. system

- How to see if you are actually making money

- How to benefit from the lessons you are learning as a Student of Commerce

- How to use your successes to improve the quality of life for yourself, your family, and the community around you.

13

The C.A.S.H. System

Aaaagh! I'm in! Now what do I do???

Well, the first thing you need to do is RELAX!

- Your stock purchases are made.

- You have calculated and faced The Worst-Case Scenario. Therefore, you have absolutely NO fear of the unknown.

- Your Initial Purchase Stop Sell is securely in place, protecting the bulk of your principal.

- You are now ready to move into a whole new dimension as a Student of Commerce.

Manage your investment with the C.A.S.H. system

You've done the hard part. You've researched, compared, watched...Then you made a decision and invested your Hard-Earned Money! Now, this is really the fun part. You get to *manage* your investment. What's that you say? You're worried that you don't have 20 years of experience as a stockbroker? No worries! Remember, **you** are a Student of Commerce!

Managing your investment is really just common sense. In the paragraphs to follow, a simple yet effective system will be laid out that will put the tools in your hands to watch over and adjust your investments for maximum profit. I call this the C.A.S.H. system. It stands for:

- *Check*

- *Adjust*

- *Sell*

- *Harvest*

Check

This step explains how you will use your Portfolio Tracking Tool to **Check** on your investments.

Adjust

As you regularly Check your investments, you will see where you want to **Adjust** your stop sells by bumping them up as the stock price rises.

Sell

You will decide ahead of time and under what conditions you will **Sell** your stock, either manually or automatically.

Harvest

After you Sell part of your investment, you will enjoy the **Harvest** of your labor.

The next four chapters will lay out, in detail, how to **Check, Adjust, Sell,** and **Harvest** your portfolio so that you maximize your profits and minimize your losses.

14
Check

Once you have real money invested in the stock market, you want to monitor your investments to see how they're doing. Your Portfolio Tracking Tool allows you to call up a website and instantly see how the values of your stocks are changing.

The great thing about the C.A.S.H. system is that you don't have to constantly be watching your investments. If you're away from your Portfolio Tracking Tool for a few hours or a few days, and the market changes drastically... you've got no worries. Your investments are on remote control.

> *"Be diligent to know the state*
> *of your flocks,*
> *And attend to your herds;*
> *For riches are not forever..."*
> *Proverbs 27:23*
>
> *The Bible, New King James Version*

When you log on to your Portfolio Tracking Tool, there is a short list of items you want to check so you will be able to clearly know the state of your "flocks and herds."

Overview of items to Check

- Check the overall market.

- Check each of the four possible combinations of Gain/Loss Today and Gain/Loss To Date:

  ➢ Gain Today and Gain To Date

  ➢ Loss Today and Gain To Date

  ➢ Gain Today and Loss To Date

  ➢ Loss Today and Loss To Date

- Check the Expiration Date of your stop sells.

- Check each stock's price over time.

- Check the historical performance of Watch List stocks.

Data elements to display in your Portfolio Tracking Tool

In order to check the items above, you will need to display certain information. Portfolio Tracking Tools vary, but you can usually configure the information that is displayed. In Chapter 9 you learned which elements to display when setting up your Watch List. You'll use the same data elements to see how the stocks you actually own are doing. You will also use the same pre-built or custom-built views in your Portfolio Tracking Tool as you did in Chapter 9 to display the following fields:

- **Symbol**
  The symbol of your stock

- **Quantity**
  How many shares of the stock you own

- **Average Purchase Cost**
  The price of each share on the date you purchased them

- **Market Price**
  The current price at which the stock is trading

- **Price Change Today**
  How much the price of your stock changed since the market opened this morning

- **Gain/Loss Today**
  Quantity times Price Change Today

- **Cost of Initial Purchase**
  How much you originally spent buying this stock

- **Current Market Value**
  Quantity times Market Price

- **Gain/Loss To Date**
  Current Market Value minus Cost of Initial Purchase

Are you logged on to your Portfolio Tracking Tool? Have you displayed the data elements you need? OK then. You're ready to Check your investments!

Check: The overall market

When you first log on to your Portfolio Tracking Tool, you need to quickly see how the market is doing. There are thousands of stocks that are traded publicly on the stock market. In an attempt to summarize how all of these stocks are doing, there are numbers that are called **indexes**. Each index has a different collection of stocks in it to represent how all of those types of stocks are doing. To keep it simple, we will only refer to three of the most widely used indexes that exist.

The Dow Jones Industrial Average

This index may also be referred to as "the DJIA", or "the Dow Jones", or just "the Dow." The Dow was created over a hundred years ago and tracks the performance of only 30 companies. However, those 30 companies are very well-established and their stocks are often referred to as "blue-chip" stocks. The Dow is the most widely referred to index.

Standard & Poor's 500

This index may also be referred to as "the S&P 500." The S&P 500 index is made up of 500 major U.S. corporations. The companies are mostly industrial firms but also have representation in the transportation, utility, and financial sectors.

NASDAQ

This is an abbreviation for "National Association of Securities Dealers Automated Quotations." The NASDAQ is really a computerized stock trading system that electronically links buyers and sellers together. There are over 5,500 stocks that are traded on the NASDAQ, and the NASDAQ Composite Index tracks them all. Many of the companies on the NASDAQ are in the technology sector. This means that, in general, if many of the technology stocks are up, the NASDAQ Composite Index will be up. Since the technology stocks are often very volatile, this index can also change quickly.

Display the Dow, S&P 500, and NASDAQ

Most Portfolio Tracking Tools automatically display several of the major indexes on their opening page so you can get a feel for the overall market as soon as you log on. If your Portfolio Tracking Tool does not display indexes, you may be able to customize the opening page or create a separate window to display the indexes.

You can also display the indexes using your charting program. Just type in the index symbol the same as you would a stock symbol. The symbols for the three indexes mentioned above are:

- $INDU or $DJI = The Dow Jones Industrial Average Index

- $COMPX = The NASDAQ Composite Index

- $INX or $SPX.X = The S&P 500 Index

Often, the major indexes will rise and fall together. If one is up, usually the others will be up and vice versa. However, indexes are compiled to track specific sectors of the market. If there was bad news in several of the technology stocks, the NASDAQ index could be down, while at the same time the Dow Jones is up.

Why check the overall market?

Checking the major indexes gives you a feel for how the market is doing today. If the Dow Jones is up 100 points, you should expect that many of the stocks you own will also be up. But the important thing is not how everyone else is doing. You want to see how **your** stocks are doing!

Check: Gain/Loss Today and Gain/Loss To Date

Go to the area of your Portfolio Tracking Tool that lists the stocks that you own. This will be titled something like "Your Portfolio" or "Account Balances" or "Positions." Let's zero in on the bottom line. Find the column that shows your **Gain/Loss Today.** Each of your stocks should have a positive (Hooray!) or negative (Grrrrgh!) number indicating how much the value of all the shares of that stock has changed since the market opened this morning. The sum of each stock's Gain/Loss Today column is your Portfolio's Total Gain or Loss for today.

Now, compare the **Gain/Loss Today** with the **Gain/Loss To Date**. Some Portfolio Tracking Tools allow you to click on columns and drag them to a new position. If yours does, try placing these two columns next to each other. Let's look at **Figure 14-1 Gain/Loss Today and To Date** to see the gains and losses in a sample portfolio. Each of the four stocks in Figure 14 represents one of the four possible combinations of Gain/Loss Today and Gain/Loss To Date.

Figure 14-1 Gain/Loss Today and To Date

	Gain/Loss Today	Gain/Loss To Date
HEYU	+ 126	+ 1,875
YME	- 202	+ 2,108
WSUP	+ 185	- 718
OHNO	- 155	- 985

Gain Today and Gain To Date

HEYU shows a positive $126 Gain/Loss Today, which means that the price of HEYU is now higher than it was when the market opened this morning. A positive $1,875 Gain/Loss To Date means that the total value of HEYU has gone up by that much since you first bought it. HEYU is up for Today **and** up To Date. This is how you wish ALL your stocks will perform. Right now, you are very pleased with your investment of HEYU.

• Why check Gain Today and Gain To Date?

Since HEYU has already made you $1,875, and your profit is increasing, you may want to move your Floating Stop Sell up to capture the additional profit the market gave you today. Floating Stop Sells will be covered in the next chapter, which explains the "A" of the C.A.S.H. system – Adjust.

Loss Today and Gain To Date

YME has a negative $202 Gain/Loss Today, which means that YME's stock price has gone down from the point at which it opened this morning. However, YME shows a positive gain of $2,108 from the day you bought it.

- Why check Loss Today and Gain To Date?

While you never like to see losses, the $202 loss today is not a whole lot of money in light of the $2,108 gain. YME may just be experiencing normal fluctuation. There's nothing to worry about right now, but keep your eye on YME. Overall, you're still very appreciative of the $2,108 gain it has given you.

Gain Today and Loss To Date

WSUP shows a positive $185 Gain/Loss Today, but To Date has lost $718. You're very grateful that today's gain makes up some of the overall loss.

- Why check Gain Today and Loss To Date?

What you **hope** is that your WSUP stock continues to increase, makes up the loss, and returns you a nice profit. Since its price has dropped, you want to continue to watch it.

Loss Today and Loss To Date

OHNO shows a loss of $155 today and a total loss of $985 since you bought it. OHNO is NOT your favorite investment right now. OHNO may be an example of The Worst-Case Scenario: you buy a stock, set an Initial Purchase Stop Sell, and then the price drops drastically. OHNO may have come dangerously close to the Initial Purchase Stop Sell several times, which means it would have sold at a loss.

- Why check Loss Today and Loss To Date?

You definitely want to closely monitor OHNO in the days to come. If it keeps going down, it will eventually hit the Trigger Price of your stop sell and sell at a loss. If you see it heading that way there are three things you can do:

> Sell at the current Market Price now to cut your loss.

> Drop the stop sell to keep it from selling now in hopes that it will rise again.

> Leave the stop sell where it is and let nature take its course.

Again, if we knew in advance what a stock's price was going to do, we'd all be rich overnight. Day in and day out, I've found it most profitable to make my best calculation on where to set the Initial Purchase Stop Sell and then leave it alone. Losses will happen. But they will be finite because you decided ahead of time what your exit strategy was. Don't fret and worry...there's lots of profit out there that will make up for this loss!

Check: The Expiration Date of your stop sells

Go to the area of your Portfolio Tracking Tool where the Orders are listed. This may be titled Open Orders, Stored Orders, or something similar. For every stock you own, you should have a companion stop sell order. When you open a stop sell order, your Online Broker will probably ask you to specify an Expiration Date. As was explained in Chapter 12, you should always pick GTC, or Good Til Canceled. This is because you want the stop sell in place until you change it yourself.

If your Online Broker accepts the GTC Expiration Date as permanent until you manually change it, then you don't have to worry about checking the Expiration Date. However, some Online Brokers accept GTC as the Expiration Date but allow the stop sell to expire after 30, or 60, or 90 days. If your Online Broker allows the stop sell to expire this way, you will need to check and make sure that each of your stop sells are not about to expire.

Every time you enter an Expiration Date for the first time, or refresh it, you should choose the latest date your broker will allow. For example, say it is May 15th when you enter your stop sell order. Let's also say that your broker allows a GTC Expiration Date up to the end of the next month. Therefore, June 30 is the latest Expiration Date you can specify.

In this example, you should choose June 30 as your stop sell order's Expiration Date. Then, mark your calendar a week before

June 30 to refresh your stop sell order's Expiration Date by extending it out to the latest date allowed. If your Online Broker has expiring stop sell orders, you will need to continually monitor your stop sells and refresh the Expiration Dates.

Why check the Expiration Date of your stop sells?

When a stop sell expires, your Online Broker cancels the stop sell order. If you had a stop sell set with a Trigger Price of $38 and it expired, the stop sell order would be canceled and you would have no protection. Then, if your stock's price plunged from $42 to $21, it would NOT sell at $38, and you would have lost profit and possibly principal. If you have a stop sell in place and it is about to expire, edit the stop sell order and enter the latest Expiration Date your Online Broker will accept.

Check: Each stock's price over time

Go to the section of your Portfolio Tracking Tool where you can call up charts of each stock. Enter your stock's symbol and then look at how its price has changed during the following time periods:

> ➢ The last 3 months

> ➢ The last 12 months

> ➢ The last 24 months

> ➢ The entire lifetime of the stock
> Some stocks will be relatively new to the market, while others may have been around for decades. Your charting program may only store data for a limited time, like 10 years. In any case, pick the period in your charting program that shows the longest time window for your stock. This may be labeled "Max" or "All Data" or something similar.

Why check each stock's price over time?

When you first found a stock with your screening program, it may have had a strong Hockey Stick shape that convinced you to invest in it. Does the stock's price trend still look like a Hockey Stick? Or, has it flattened out or turned downward? If so, has the stock's price done this before? That's the advantage of looking at the long-term price trend of your stock.

For example, let's say that in August, you found a stock whose price from January through July was in the shape of a strong Hockey Stick. You decide to buy that stock. In December, you look at your stock's price and notice that in November and December, the stock's price has flattened out. The stock's price trend that once looked like a Hockey Stick now looks like it got caught in a car door and bent.

You wonder if you ought to go ahead and sell the stock and invest your money in another stock whose price is appreciating. But before you decide, you look at the 10-year price chart of your stock. What you see is that every November and December the price flattens out, but then starts sloping up again in January. This could be an annual trend that is caused by low demand for the company's services during the holidays. Knowing this, you may decide to hold on to your stock until after the first of the year and see if the historical trend repeats itself and rewards you with more profit.

Check: Historical performance of Watch List stocks

The stocks in your Watch Lists are there because they passed the screening criteria discussed in Chapter 9. The stocks in your Alpha Stocks List are ones that you have graduated from any one of your possible Watch Lists because their performance has impressed you and you are considering buying them. Some of the stocks in your Alpha Stocks List will be chosen to go on your Stocks To Buy Worksheet from which you will make your purchases.

You will continue to use the same skills you've already developed to Check for new candidates to put on the Stocks To Buy Worksheet when the time is right. You will want to run the following Checks on all of the stocks in your Alpha Stocks List and each of the Watch Lists you have created.

Sort to see gains and losses of Watch List stocks

- Click on the Gain/Loss To Date column to sort the gains or losses for each stock so that the biggest number is at the top.

If you spent the same amount of Play Money on each stock in your Watch List, you can quickly see which stock would have given you the most return.

- You can also see how the stocks in your Watch List are doing compared to each other by sorting on columns with names like:

  ➤ Monthly Percentage Gain

  ➤ Price Change over 6 Months

  ➤ Percentage Gain To Date

Re-evaluate the Watch List stocks' prices over time

When you originally researched the stocks to put in your Watch List, you looked at their price trends over time. You learned to look for a steady slope upward over the last three to nine months, resulting in a Hockey Stick shape. Now that these stocks have been in your Watch List for some time, has the price continued to trend upward? Or, once you bought shares with Play Money, did the price drop or flatten out?

Why check historical performance of Watch List stocks?

One day soon, you will be ready to purchase more stocks. If the price of a stock on your Watch List has continued to slope up, you might want to move it on to the Alpha Stocks List. This way, you will always have a "hot list" of stocks to choose from once you are ready to buy again.

Summary

- Check the overall market.

- Check each of the four possible combinations of Gain/Loss Today and Gain/Loss To Date:

  ➢ Gain Today and Gain To Date

  ➢ Loss Today and Gain To Date

  ➢ Gain Today and Loss To Date

  ➢ Loss Today and Loss To Date

- Check the Expiration Date of your stop sells.

- Check each stock's price over time.

- Check the historical performance of Watch List stocks.

15
Adjust

*"It's tough to make predictions,
especially about the future."*

**Yogi Berra (1925 -)
American Baseball Player**

The previous chapter outlined at least nine items every good Student of Commerce should Check periodically. As you know by now, the Check is the "C" of the C.A.S.H. system. Now it's time to learn about the "A" of the C.A.S.H system – **Adjust.**

The C.A.S.H. system was designed for Students of Commerce like you – individuals with families, Day Jobs, and hobbies. One reason that makes it so easy to use is that it doesn't require you to be glued to your computer monitor, watching every tick of a stock's price as it goes up or down. In fact, there is actually only one item that you will need to Adjust:

The Floating Stop Sell

In Chapter 10, the stop sell was introduced as a tool to protect your principal investment and to capture the appreciated value of your stocks. At the end of the chapter, you learned that you would use two different types of stop sells to accomplish this:

➢ The Initial Purchase Stop Sell, and

➢ The Floating Stop Sell

In Chapter 11, you learned how to calculate the Trigger Price of the Initial Purchase Stop Sell for every one of the stocks you own. When you purchased each of your stocks, you created an Initial Purchase Stop Sell to protect the bulk of your principal. Once the stock's price rises above the purchase price and stays there for several days, you will convert the Initial Purchase Stop Sell to a Floating Stop Sell.

Look at the graph of HEYU's price over time in **Figure 15-1 Progression of a Floating Stop Sell**. The history of HEYU's stock price is shown as a straight line that starts at $35 in June and goes to more than $50 in September. Of course, real stock prices are never a straight line, but I took this liberty to show the Floating Stop Sell concept more clearly. You can see that HEYU was purchased for $40 per share in late June. The Initial Purchase Stop Sell was set with a Trigger Price of $36.

Figure 15-1 Progression of a Floating Stop Sell

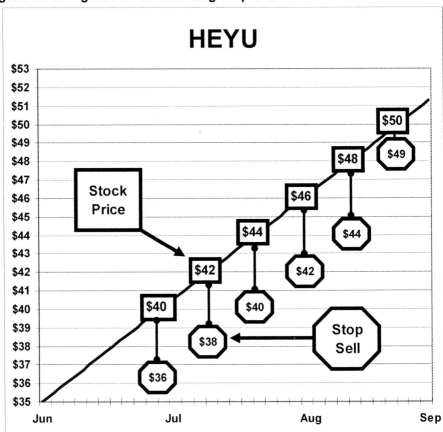

Back in Chapter 11, you learned how to determine the Average Day Range and the Biggest Price Drop of a stock. These numbers were used to determine where to set the Initial Purchase Stop Sell. You will use these same numbers to help you decide how close you want to "Float" to the Market Price.

In Chapter 11, it was determined that the Average Day Range was $3 and the Biggest Price Drop was $4. With these numbers in mind, the Initial Purchase Stop Sell was set at $4 below the current Market Price, which at the time was $40. Therefore, the Initial Purchase Stop Sell was set at $40 minus $4, or $36. For now, let's keep that same $4 buffer between the Market Price and the Floating Stop Sell.

In early July, HEYU's stock price goes up to $42. Once it does, you feel confident in moving your Initial Purchase Stop Sell of $36 up $2 to $38. The way to do that is to go into your Online Broker and find the stop sell you set up as the Initial Purchase Stop Sell for HEYU. The Trigger Price is still set at $36. You should be able to edit the stop sell and change the Trigger Price from $36 to $38.

Important Note!

In Chapter 5, it was pointed out that you should choose an Online Broker that does NOT charge you to place or edit a stop sell order.

Make sure that is the case and then feel free to create, cancel, or change stop sells as often as you like.

Once you have changed the Trigger Price to $38, review and accept the transaction. Then, go back to where your Online Broker lists pending orders and make sure that the stop sell is now set at $38.

You just converted your **Initial Purchase Stop Sell** of $36 to a **Floating Stop Sell** of $38. From now on, the stop sell that protects the bulk of your principal will be called a Floating Stop Sell. Let's talk about that protection for a minute. What if HEYU's price dropped to $28 after you set the Floating Stop Sell to $38? Your Online Broker would put your shares of HEYU up for sale and within a few seconds they would be bought at the current Market Price. This should be within a few cents of your $38 Trigger Price.

You bought HEYU at $40 and it sold at $38. You would lose $2 times the number of HEYU shares you own. However, you were protected from the disastrous drop in price from $42 to $28. You will have this type of loss sometimes, and it hurts. But as you learn how to buy stronger and stronger Hockey Sticks, your losses will be less and less.

If there is a drastic price drop, you **hope** that you have been able to bump up your Floating Stop Sell far enough to protect your principal. For example, when HEYU's price hits $44, you can move your Floating Stop Sell up to $40 which is what you bought HEYU for. NOW, if there is a drastic price drop, your entire principal is protected. From this point on, it's all profit!

When HEYU's price goes to $46, you move the Floating Stop Sell to $42. Now if the stock's price drops past $42, your Floating Stop Sell will sell your stocks at $42. The great news is, you made a $2 profit between the $40 purchase price and the $42 sales price on every share! The same scenario happens at a price of $48. You move the Floating Stop Sell up to $44 and enjoy a $4 per share profit if it sells.

Now look at the $50 marker in Figure 15-1. When HEYU hits $50, you are delighted to have made $10 per share! If you kept the Floating Stop Sell Trigger Price the same amount below the Market Price as you have been doing, you would set it at $46. However, say that HEYU has been at $50 for some time now. You may be ready to cash in on the profit you've made and either spend some of it or invest it in another stock that has a strong Hockey Stick shape. Instead of setting the Floating Stop Sell at $46, you set it at $49. That way, if HEYU takes off and climbs higher, you can enjoy even more profit. But if it misbehaves and dips down past $49 – Whammy! It sells and you have a bucket of cash! That's the great advantage of the Floating Stop Sell. You can adjust it as close or as far away from the Market Price as you want.

Do I ever want to Adjust my Floating Stop Sell down?

The short answer is: Hardly ever.

The whole point of the C.A.S.H. system is that you don't have to constantly monitor and worry about your investments! As you watch your stock's price drop, you may be tempted to move your stop sell down. There are only a few times when this is a good idea. The only reason to move a Floating Stop Sell down is if, upon careful scrutiny, you strongly feel that you set it too high. An example of this might be if the Average Day Range is $3 and you set your stop sell only $1.50 under the Market Price. As the price started to decline, you realize you didn't give the stock's price enough room to move around naturally without triggering the stop sell. In that case, you might adjust it down to $3 under the Market Price.

You can drive yourself crazy adjusting a stop sell every half hour. Unless you think you really messed up on where you set the stop sell...***Leave it alone!*** When I'm at my Day Job and have a 15-minute break in the morning, I may go to a computer and pull up my Portfolio Tracking Tool to **Check** on my stocks. If I see that the market is down and all of my stocks are going down in price, I'll review my stop sells just to make sure they are safely in place. Then I log off.

On my lunch break, I'll log back on to my Portfolio Tracking Tool and see how things are going. If my stocks are still going down, I will log off and not check my Portfolio Tracking Tool again that day. Why?

- There is nothing I can do to change how the stock's prices are moving.

- Pulling up my Portfolio Tracking Tool every 15 minutes to watch a declining market is no fun.

- I refuse to worry. Worrying burns up precious brain cycles and brings nothing positive into your life.

- I have already made my decision. I gave my Best Effort calculating the stop sells. Now, I'm going to stand confidently by and let the market take its course. I'm fearless! I'm a Student of Commerce!

So, are your stock's prices falling? No problem. Log off. Turn your back. Walk away. Go and invest your time in the infinite number of issues where you **can** make a difference. Encourage a co-worker. Call your spouse or kids and tell them how special they are to you. Don't worry about your portfolio. The market will go up and down. But you have the distinct advantage of having the C.A.S.H. system working for you!

Summary

- As your stock's price rises from your purchase price, you will raise the Initial Purchase Stop Sell.

- Raising the Initial Purchase Stop Sell converts it to a Floating Stop Sell.

- Your first objective is to get the Floating Stop Sell above the stock's purchase price.

- Once the Floating Stop Sell is above the purchase price, your entire principal is protected!

- As the stock's price continues to rise, you will incrementally raise the Floating Stop Sell to capture the growing profit.

- Resist the temptation to lower your Floating Stop Sell.

16
Sell

In Chapter 14, you learned that the "C" of the C.A.S.H. system stood for how you **Check** your portfolio.

In Chapter 15, the "A" of the C.A.S.H. system represented items that you will **Adjust** in your portfolio.

In this Chapter, the "S" of the C.A.S.H. system will represent methods to **Sell** your stocks.

How do I sell stocks?

There are only two ways that you will sell stocks that you own and are in your portfolio.

- Automatically, via stop sells

- Manually

Automatic sale of stocks

The majority of your stock sales will be done automatically using the Initial Purchase Stop Sell and the Floating Stop Sell. This method is one of the strongest benefits of the C.A.S.H. system. Predetermining the conditions under which you will sell a stock and having it happen automatically eliminates all of the stress of fretting about when to press the "Sell" button. It also requires much less emotional involvement.

Let your Floating Stop Sell do the dirty work

Let's say that after you bought shares in YME, they increased in price nicely for three months. Then, during the fourth month, the price didn't change up or down more than a few cents. In the meantime, there is a stock on your Alpha Stocks List that has a perfect Hockey Stick price trend and has been steadily increasing. You are appreciative of the nice returns YME has generated, but if it isn't going to increase any more, you would rather use your money to buy that stock on your Alpha Stocks List. On the other hand, if YME took off again, you would like to be there to collect even more profit. What to do?

You could issue a Market Order to sell your shares of YME and be done with it. Or, you could move your Floating Stop Sell to within a few cents of YME's current Market Price. That way, if YME's price takes off again, you still own the shares and make even more money. But if it drops more than a few cents, the decision is made for you and it sells! You are left with a nice bucket of money to invest in that promising stock on your Alpha Stocks List. Bottom line: the more you can automate your sales, the better. However, there are times when you want to take your portfolio off cruise control and take direct control.

Manual sale of stocks

With the C.A.S.H. system, you are always in control. It's your Hard-Earned Money, and you are an educated Student of Commerce who is trained to make productive, timely decisions. You can manually sell as many of your stocks as often as you want. Let's consider some reasons why you might want to do just that.

Why would I manually sell stocks?

You're ready to take your profit and move on

In the late 1990s, I owned shares in a stock that started appreciating the day I bought it. The chart of the price history for this stock was a classic Hockey Stick shape. It just kept going up and up and up. This went on for months. I did **not** want to set my Floating Stop Sell close to the Market Price and risk selling all of the shares. I felt like that would be killing the goose that laid the golden egg. But I did want some cash! So, every now and then, I would issue a Market Order to sell just a few of the shares. As soon as the shares sold, the cash was deposited in my Online Broker account, and I would withdraw it just like I would from my bank savings account. Sometimes, you want to sell some shares **now**. And that's OK, because it's **your** Hard-Earned Money!

A stock starts misbehaving

Sometimes a stock's price trend goes from the shape of a smooth, well-defined Hockey Stick to the shape of steep mountains and valleys. If this happens, you may feel that the stock no longer qualifies to have the honor of being in your elite portfolio. Again, you're the boss, and **you** get to decide who plays on your team. You have a responsibility to protect your Hard-Earned Money, and if a stock disqualifies itself in your eyes, it has to go. You can execute a Market Order to Sell or move the Floating Stop Sell so close to the Market Price that if it burps in the wrong direction, it's history. (Or actually, cash!)

New info

Once I bought a stock in a company without researching it thoroughly. Right away, the stock started appreciating in price and making a nice profit. One day I was watching TV and learned that a product made by that company conflicted with our family's values.

It was late at night, and the stock market had closed hours ago. I immediately logged on to my Online Broker and issued a Market Order to sell all of the shares of the stock. Executing a Market Order when the market was closed violated one of the principles I've stated in this book...never execute a Market Order when the market is closed. It didn't matter. I was not going to hold shares of stock in a company whose product was dangerous to my family.

Bad news

Sometimes you'll hear bad news about a company whose stock you own. Bad news doesn't always mean the price of the company's stock will go down. If that is what you're worried about, maybe all you need to do is tighten up your Floating Stop Sell and let the market do what the market is going to do.

However, if you have bad vibes about owning that company, it's your call. Execute a Market Order to Sell and move on. Life is too short to worry.

How to manually sell a stock

If you want to manually sell any of your stocks, the process is almost identical to placing a Market Order to Buy as explained in Chapter 12.

Important Note!

In order to manually sell a stock, your Online Broker may require you to first cancel any stop sells you have in place for that stock.

This is because your Online Broker may not allow you to have orders to sell more shares of a stock than you actually own. If this is the case, simply go to the area of your Online Broker where the stop sell orders are listed. Delete the stop sell of the stock you want to manually sell. Now you may proceed with the manual sale of your stock. Log on to your Online Broker and go to the Order Entry screen. Fill in the screen with the following values:

- **Action:**
  Select **Sell.**

- **Quantity**
  Enter the number of shares you want to sell. You can enter any number from one to the total number you own.

- **Symbol:**
  Enter the symbol of the stock you want to sell.

- **Order type:**
  Select **Market.**

Once you confirm that the order is correct, click the button to execute the transaction. Within a few seconds, your stocks will be sold and the cash value will be deposited into your Online Broker account.

Summary

- Automatically selling your stocks ensures that:

  ➢ The majority of your stock sales are done via the stop sells you set up, and

  ➢ Your Floating Stop Sell does the dirty work when you want to get rid of a stock.

- Why you would manually sell stocks:

  ➢ You're ready to take your profit and move on

  ➢ A stock starts misbehaving

  ➢ You get new info about the stock

  ➢ You get bad news regarding the company

17
Harvest

At this point, the C.A.S.H. system has taught you how to **Check** the condition of your portfolio, **Adjust** your Floating Stop Sells in order to protect your principal and capture profit, and defined how and when to **Sell** your stocks.

The "H" of the C.A.S.H. system stands for **Harvest**.

Investing in the stock market is much like planting a garden. When you purchase a stock, it is like taking a seed and putting it in the ground. Your hope for that seed is that it takes root and breaks through the surface of the earth. This is what you hope for each of your stocks; that they will take hold at the time of your purchase and go up in a few days. Once a seedling is through the crust of the earth, it has a better chance of surviving. It's the same with your investment. Once it has increased in price over your purchase price, you can get your Floating Stop Sell under it so that your principal is protected.

In the garden, some of the seeds never get established enough to grow. Some will die in the ground. Unfortunately, it will be the same with some of your investments. Regardless of how hard you study a stock before you buy it, some will never grow past your purchase price but will "die in the ground" by triggering your Initial Purchase Stop Sell. It will be the minority of the "seeds" you "plant", but it will happen to some.

In the garden, the longer a seedling grows, the stronger it gets. Eventually, it becomes mature and produces its fruit or Harvest. Most of your stock purchases will do the same. They will grow in price, and the taller they grow away from your purchase price, the more profit, or Harvest, you will have.

Some of your investments will grow for a long time, like the mighty redwood trees. These are great stocks to have in your portfolio because as they grow toward the sun, the value of your portfolio is growing. Other investments will be like the plants that only grow a short time, bloom, and then are done. Armed with your Floating Stop Sells, you'll be able to follow these stocks all the way up to their full maturity. Then, when their season is over and they "die", your Floating Stop Sell will automatically reap the Harvest.

As you invest, you will be purchasing stocks at various times. If you had a garden, and every so many days, you went out and put a few more seeds in it, the garden would have plants in all different stages of the maturity cycle. You would have some seeds that were still trying to break ground and get established. Other seedlings would have broken ground but would still be very small. Some would be in a strong growth phase and getting taller every day, while others would look like their growth was stunted. Every few days, only some of the plants would be ready to harvest.

Keeping the garden analogy in mind will help you better manage the stocks in your portfolio. Every stock will be in its own unique growth cycle, will mature at a different rate, and be ready for Harvesting at a different time. Unfortunately, some of your stocks will not "break ground" and others will be picked off by the "vultures" of the economic market. Then there will be the prize plants that confidently grow strong and bloom into a beautiful harvest.

What do I do with my Harvest – Cash!

As the stocks in your portfolio "garden" mature, you will Harvest them and produce a cash crop of, well....Cash! This is the payday you have been working toward in your New Part-Time Job. You, of course, absolutely get to decide how you're going to spend the cash in your Online Broker account. Here are the two basic paths you can take on deciding the destiny of your Harvest:

- Withdraw it and spend it

- Re-invest it

Withdrawing cash from your Online Brokerage account

It is a simple process to take some of your Harvest cash out of your Online Brokerage account and put it into your pocket. At your local neighborhood bank, if you wanted money from your savings account, you would go to the branch bank, fill out a withdrawal slip, and present it to the teller. The teller would then give you the funds in either cash or a paper document such as a bank cashier's check.

The process for taking cash out of your Online Broker is much the same. However, chances are that your Online Broker does **not** have a branch in your town, so you will have to execute the transaction online or over the phone. Once you fill out the proper withdrawal documents, your Online Broker can either mail you a paper check or electronically deposit the funds into another financial institution like your local bank or a credit union.

How much cash should I withdraw?

Of course it's your Hard-Earned Money, so you can take out as much or as little as you want. Here are some things to think about.

- Since you are a disciplined Student of Commerce, it is always best to withdraw and spend your cash according to a pre-determined plan. You could just withdraw $1,000 from your Online Brokerage account and plop it into your bank checking account. If you did that without a plan on how to spend it, chances are that in a couple of months you would be hard pressed to say what you spent your Hard-Earned Money on. Here are some sample financial objectives you might want to have for your investment Harvest:

  - ➢ Pay off credit card debt

  - ➢ Pay off automobile or school loans

  - ➢ Pay cash for a family vacation

  - ➢ Pay the mortgage off early

- The more cash you leave in your Online Brokerage account, the more you will have to re-invest. This leads us to the second possible destiny for your Harvest.

Re-investing your cash

Whenever any of your stocks sell, cash will be deposited into your Online Brokerage account. As we discussed in the previous section, you can withdraw those funds to spend as you like. The money left in your account can be re-invested by purchasing additional stocks. As you begin to make your plans on how to re-invest your cash, consider the following:

Cash management principles

- Principle #1 - Cash sitting in your Online Brokerage account isn't going to earn the kind of returns you want.

- Principle #2 - Take your time re-investing. Don't let Principle #1 panic you or get you in a hurry.

Principle #1 and Principle #2 should both be applied to your re-investment strategy so that you make a balanced decision. If you have a bucket of money in your account and ignore it for 5 weeks, you would be missing out on 10% of the investment opportunity for the entire year. On the other hand, you don't want a cash balance in your account to pressure you to make a hasty purchase decision you will regret later. Take your time and fully exercise the research techniques taught in this book.

The market may have recently fallen dramatically and all of your stop sells executed. You may have fewer shares of stock and mostly cash. Hey, relax! Let things settle down. Do more research. Become a better Student of Commerce. The market will be there when you're ready. You are in control. You ARE NOT a victim of the stock market. You are employing the stock market to accumulate wealth.

Always be ready to re-plant your Harvest

In Chapter 14, you learned that you should regularly Check the Watch Lists in your Portfolio Tracking Tool. Also, your Alpha Stocks List should always have two to six stocks that are good candidates to purchase. When it's time to re-invest, you will do a final check on these stocks to see if you still think they are good choices for investing your Hard-Earned Money. Remember to fill in your Stocks To Buy Worksheet so that you can calculate what Initial Purchase Stop Sell you want to create for each purchase. Then, when the market is open, place your Market Order to Buy, followed immediately by your Initial Purchase Stop Sell.

You will then start the Check, Adjust, Sell, and Harvest cycles of the C.A.S.H. system over again. By following this process, you will continually be planting new seed in your investment garden, watching your investments grow and develop, and then harvesting them to enjoy financial rewards.

Summary

- Your investment portfolio is like a garden.

- When your investments are mature, you will Harvest them by selling them and generating cash.

- Once you have cash in your Online Brokerage account, you will either:

  ➤ Withdraw it, or

  ➤ Re-invest it

- It's best to have a plan for how you will spend the cash that you withdraw, so that you have something to show for the Hard-Earned Money you earned through investing.

- Cash Management Principles

  ➤ Principle #1 - Cash sitting in your Online Brokerage account isn't going to earn the kind of returns you want.

  ➤ Principle #2 - Take your time re-investing. Don't let Principle #1 panic you or get you in a hurry.

- Always be ready to re-plant your Harvest by continually reviewing your Alpha Stocks List for stocks that have impressed you with their performance.

18

How Do I Know if
I'm Making Money?

You have diligently researched stocks and put them in your Watch List. You've been making purchases of stocks and creating a companion Initial Purchase Stop Sell for each one. You've also been carefully watching the stock appreciate in price, and you have adjusted the Floating Stop Sell so that you protect your principal and capture profit. Some of your stocks have dropped in price, triggered your stop sell, and deposited cash into your Online Broker account. You've taken some money out and re-invested some of it into more stocks. You have embraced and executed all of the techniques of the C.A.S.H. system. The question you may have now is, **"Am I making any money doing this?"**

Congratulations! That is exactly the kind of question an experienced and mature Student of Commerce **should** be asking. You have worked too hard at your New Part-Time Job to be doing all this and not making a profit. So, how do you know? There is only one way – Metrics!

What are metrics?

- Met·rics (mĕt'rĭks) n. A standard of measurement; the application of statistics and mathematical analysis to a specified field

- Metrics define what is to be measured.

- These measurements, or metrics, can be used to track trends, productivity, resources, and much more.

- Typically, the metrics tracked are key performance indicators.

Simply stated, metrics are numbers and statistics that allow you to measure something. In your case, you want to measure the profitability of your investments.

You want your metrics to work for you so that they tell a story. Each metric will have different information so that you can see different "views" of the data. Between what your Portfolio Tracking Tool can display and what you can calculate on your own, there is an infinite variety of numbers that can represent your portfolio. You want to be careful that you don't have so much data that it is overwhelming and discourages you. This chapter will show you how to calculate a few key indicators that will tell you the story about how successful your investments are.

Metrics for the stocks you currently own

The chart in **Figure 18-1 Performance Metrics of Stocks Currently Owned** shows individual stocks and numbers associated with those stocks. Figure 18-1 will represent stocks that you have purchased and which are in your portfolio. The purpose of this profitability analysis is to see how much the stocks you purchased have increased or decreased in value. Your Portfolio Tracking Tool will be able to display most, if not all, of these numbers. However, I recommend that at first you get a notepad, calculator, and pencil and crunch the numbers yourself. This will give you confidence and understanding about what your Portfolio Tracking Tool is showing you.

You can download the spreadsheet shown in Figure 18-1 for your own use at www.ChrisHart1.com.

Figure 18-1 Performance Metrics of Stocks Currently Owned

Stock Symbol	Shares Owned	Purchase Price	Market Price	$ Profit Per Share	% Profit Per Share	$ Profit ALL Shares
HEYU	260	$ 38.94	$ 46.45	$ 7.51	19.29%	$ 1,952.60
YME	82	$ 65.40	$ 72.68	$ 7.28	11.13%	$ 596.96
WSUP	400	$ 43.15	$ 42.57	$ (0.58)	-1.34%	$ (232.00)
OHNO	180	$ 54.13	$ 51.27	$ (2.86)	-5.28%	$ (514.80)

Stock Symbol	Purchase Date	Today's Date	Days Owned	Daily R.O.I.	Annual R.O.I.
HEYU	03/09/2012	10/29/2012	234	0.0824%	30.08%
YME	04/27/2012	10/29/2012	185	0.0602%	21.96%
OHNO	06/01/2012	10/29/2012	150	-0.0090%	-3.27%
WSUP	02/03/2012	10/29/2012	269	-0.0196%	-7.17%

Here's a column-by-column breakdown of the labels used in Figure 18-1.

- **Stock Symbol**
  The symbol of the stock you own

- **Shares Owned**
  The number of shares of the stock you own

- **Purchase Price**
  The price of each share on the date you purchased it

- **Market Price**
  The current price at which the stock is trading

- **$ Profit Per Share**
  Market Price minus Purchase Price

- **% Profit Per Share**
  $ Profit Per Share divided by Purchase Price

- **$ Profit ALL Shares**
  Shares Owned times $ Profit Per Share

- **Purchase Date**
  The date you purchased the stock

- **Today's Date**
  The date today

- **Days Owned**

  This is Today's Date minus Purchase Date. Spreadsheets do a great job of calculating the number of days between two dates. If you are calculating this manually, you may need to look at a calendar to count the number of days between your Purchase Date and Today's Date. It is important that this number be accurate because the value of Days Owned will affect the next two metrics.

- **Daily R.O.I.**

  The Daily R.O.I. is the average daily return on investment each stock has produced since you purchased it. It is calculated from % Profit Per Share divided by Days Owned. This number will usually be a small fractional number. In Figure 18-1, it is expressed as a percent with four positions to the right of the decimal. The most important reason for calculating the Daily R.O.I. is so that you can calculate the Annual R.O.I.

- **Annual R.O.I.**

  The Annual R.O.I. is the Daily R.O.I. times 365. This shows what your return on investment would be if you owned the stock for exactly one year.

What do these metrics tell me?

$ Profit Per Share

This is the dollar amount your investment has changed per share. While the $ Profit Per Share metric is interesting, a $4 change on a $20 stock is much more significant than a $4 change on a $150 stock. That's why we calculate the next metric.

% Profit Per Share

By calculating the change in stock price as a percentage, you can see how each stock's performance compares with the other stocks in your portfolio. This gives you a standardized view of each stock's performance regardless of how high or low each share's price is.

$ Profit ALL Shares

This gives you a feel for how big a bucket of money you made on each stock.

Days Owned

This number, when compared with the other profit numbers, gives you a sense of how fast you made the profit that you did.

Daily R.O.I.

Since these numbers are such small fractions, it is hard to get much of a picture of what they represent. The main purpose of calculating the Daily R.O.I. is to have a number to calculate the Annual R.O.I.

Annual R.O.I.

This is one of the most important metrics you can calculate for your stocks. Once you have the Annual R.O.I. calculated, you can compare what you made in the stock market with other financial instruments, such as bank certificates of deposit, annuities, and even mutual funds. In Figure 18-1, your investment in HEYU made $1,952.60. While that's not a huge amount of money, the fact that it calculates out to 30.08% Annual R.O.I. is fantastic. When you compare 30.08% from your HEYU investment to a return on a bank certificate of deposit of less than 5%, you start to smile and pat yourself on the back for buying this stock.

Metrics for the stocks you have sold

The chart in Figure 18-1 gives you different views on the profitability of the stocks you currently own. Another important analysis is to calculate the profitability of the stocks you bought and sold. The numbers in **Figure 18-2 Performance Metrics of Stocks Once Owned, Now Sold** are very similar to those in Figure 18-1. The math is the same, but two of the columns are titled differently to represent stocks that you have **sold** instead of stocks that you currently **own**. The columns in Figure 18-2 that are different from Figure 18-1 are:

Sale Price (instead of Market Price)

This column is where you record the price at which you sold the stock. Your Online Broker should allow you to review historical transactions. Using this feature, you can go back to any transaction and look up the price at which the stock sold.

Sale Date (instead of Today's Date)

This column is where you record the date you sold the stock. When you access the historical transactions in your Online Broker, you should be able to see the Sale Date in the same place you find the Sale Price.

Figure 18-2 Performance Metrics of Stocks Once Owned, Now Sold

Stock Symbol	Shares Owned	Purchase Price	Sale Price	$ Profit Per Share	% Profit Per Share	$ Profit ALL Shares
SOLD1	61	$ 45.45	$ 62.15	$ 16.70	36.75%	$ 1,018.78
SOLD2	100	$ 69.27	$ 64.21	$ (5.06)	-7.31%	$ (506.04)
SOLD3	200	$ 12.60	$ 15.11	$ 2.51	19.88%	$ 501.08
SOLD4	100	$ 38.93	$ 42.65	$ 3.72	9.54%	$ 371.59
SOLD5	255	$ 29.41	$ 31.89	$ 2.48	8.43%	$ 632.40

Stock Symbol	Purchase Date	Sale Date	Days Owned	Daily R.O.I.	Annual R.O.I.
SOLD1	10/19/2009	01/11/2010	84	0.4375%	159.68%
SOLD2	09/11/2009	01/25/2010	136	-0.0537%	-19.61%
SOLD3	08/17/2009	04/07/2010	233	0.0853%	31.15%
SOLD4	04/01/2010	05/24/2010	53	0.1801%	65.73%
SOLD5	04/27/2010	06/10/2010	44	0.1916%	69.95%

"Sold1" through "Sold5" are fictitious names representing stocks you have bought and sold.

Metrics for the overall value of your portfolio

The chart in Figure 18-1 showed you how profitable each of the stocks that you purchased are today. The chart in Figure 18-2 showed you how much profit you made on stocks that you purchased and then sold. Another important view into the profitability of your portfolio is how much the total value of your portfolio has changed.

Your Portfolio Tracking Tool will probably have a feature that shows you this view of your profitability. When you're getting started, I recommend that you calculate all of the numbers yourself. There's just something about sitting down with a calculator, pencil, and pad of paper that helps you really wrap your arms around your numbers. Figure 18-3 Change in Portfolio Value is a chart with a very simple view of your portfolio's change in profitability.

Figure 18-3 Change in Portfolio Value

	Date	Value of All Stocks	Cash Balance	Total Portfolio Value
Monday	03/05/2012	$ 12,342	$ 25	$ 12,367
Tuesday	03/06/2012	$ 12,661	$ 25	$ 12,686
Wednesday	03/07/2012	$ 12,926	$ 25	$ 12,951
Thursday	03/08/2012	$ 10,926	$ 2,190	$ 13,116
Friday	03/09/2012	$ 10,952	$ 2,190	$ 13,142
Monday	03/12/2012	$ 13,037	$ 86	$ 13,123
Tuesday	03/13/2012	$ 12,982	$ 86	$ 13,067
Wednesday	03/14/2012	$ 12,914	$ 86	$ 12,999
Thursday	03/15/2012	$ 13,047	$ 86	$ 13,132
Friday	03/16/2012	$ 13,465	$ 86	$ 13,551

Date

If you record your portfolio's value every day, you can roll up the data into higher-level summaries such as weekly or monthly. Your schedule may prevent you from accessing your Portfolio Tracking Tool every day to view and log your portfolio's value. If you miss some days, you should be able to access either your Portfolio Tracking Tool or your Online Broker to get the historical value of your portfolio.

Value of All Stocks

When you're recording the value of your stocks over a period of days, it is important to take the reading at the same time every day. The simplest way to achieve this consistency is to record the value of all your stocks after the close of the market. If you get the historical value of all your stocks from your Portfolio Tracking Tool, that number **will be** after the close of the market. The Value of All Stocks number is simply the Current Market Value of all of the shares of all of the stocks you currently own.

Cash Balance

As you buy and sell stocks, the Cash Balance in your Online Brokerage account will change. It's good to track this number because it will remind you how much you have to spend on new stocks when it is time to buy more. You want to be sure and add it to the Total Portfolio Value so you get an accurate picture of all of your investment assets. Notice how the cash balance changed in Figure 18-3:

➢ On Monday, March 5, there was only $25 in cash in the Online Brokerage account. This is because the investor had used almost all of his cash to buy stocks.

➢ On Thursday, March 8, the Value of All Stocks went down approximately $2,000, and the Cash Balance went up approximately $2,000. This could have been caused by a price drop in one of the stocks in the portfolio, which then triggered a Floating Stop Sell. That would result in the sale of the stock for about $2,000 and the subsequent deposit of that amount of cash.

➢ On Friday, March 9, the $2,190 remained in the account.

➢ On Monday, March 12, $2,104 was spent on buying new stocks. This left a Cash Balance of $86 and increased the Value of All Stocks by more than $2,000.

Total Portfolio Value

This is the sum of the Value of All Stocks plus Cash Balance. What you hope to see is that your portfolio's value is increasing over time.

To make it real, write it down!

Documenting your profitability can sometimes be painful as you come face to face with the losses you've had. It will also be a reality check on how good you're actually doing overall as an investor. And, when you're knocking it out of the park, it will be a tangible report card that verifies the great job you've been doing as a Student of Commerce.

However well accomplished you've become at investing, you can always do better. That's one of the stimulating benefits of being a Student of Commerce. There is always something else to learn. Learning from your own experience is one of the best ways to improve your skills as an investor. The next chapter will lay out techniques for capturing your valuable life experience and using it to go to the next level.

Summary

- Metrics are numbers and statistics that allow you to measure the profitability of your investments.

- You will want to calculate and track some simple metrics to document how profitable your investments are.

- To see how profitable your current stocks are, calculate:

  - ➤ $ Profit Per Share

  - ➤ % Profit Per Share

  - ➤ $ Profit ALL Shares

  - ➤ Days Owned

  - ➤ Annual R.O.I.

- To see how profitable the stocks you bought and sold were, calculate the same metrics as you do for the stocks you currently own. The only difference is that you use:

  - ➤ Sale Price instead of Market Price

  - ➤ Sale Date instead of Today's Date

- To see how profitable your overall portfolio is, keep a daily log of:

  - ➤ Value of All Stocks

  - ➤ Cash Balance

  - ➤ Total Portfolio (Value of All Stocks plus Cash Balance)

19

What Have I Learned, and What Am I Going to Do About It?

Your own experience is the very best teacher

Once you've actually spent your Hard-Earned Money on a stock, watched it rise or fall in price, and then sold it at a profit or loss, you have an experience that far surpasses textbook theory. It's important that you capture that experience and learn from it. You may think, "Oh, I'll never forget that lesson!" Then, as life goes on and thousands of other thoughts compete for your memory, that valuable life experience may well slip away. How do you keep that from happening? Write it down!

Start a log

Capturing your thoughts, ideas, questions, and revelations can be a very simple process. You don't need fancy computer models to enter your data into. I'd suggest starting with a notepad and a three ring binder. That way, as you make notes on the notepad, you can tear the pages off and put them in the binder.

- You should have a separate page for each stock you own. If your notes grow, and you have multiple pages, you can get a set of tabs that go in your binder so you can easily find each stock's section.

- Encourage your creativity by keeping free-form notes. Don't limit yourself to a rigid structure. Allow your notes to take any form you want. If you want to jot down the date when your stock dropped $20 and then next to it, draw a sad face with horns – do it! Record your thoughts, concerns, and excitement about how the stock is performing. Here are some ideas on comments you might want to jot down for a stock:

> ➤ "Dipped $5 this week. Has dipped this much before but always goes back up."

> ➤ "Flat for a month. If not up next week, creep Floating Stop Sell to within $1 of Market Price."

> ➤ "Performs well in summer. Be ready to capture profit on price jump this June."

> ➤ "Doesn't look like it will go above purchase price. Sell now, take loss, and run?"

> ➤ "Once price goes up another $1, move Floating Stop Sell to Purchase Price. Then I'm home safe!"

These kinds of comments will give you perspective and confidence about your next move. The more comments you log about each stock, the better!

What did I learn from my last transaction?

We've all heard the expression, "Hindsight is 20/20." While you can't change the past, evaluating what you would have done differently is very valuable. One of the best ways I know to do this is to draw a picture.

Figure 19-1 Evaluation of Purchase and Sale of a Stock shows the price history of stock XYZ from April through August. The comments on Figure 19-1 represent the analysis you can do on each of your transactions. This process can be as simple as printing out the price chart and then making your comments with a pen. You can then add the marked-up printout to your binder, along with the other information you may have about that stock. Your Portfolio Tracking Tool might allow you to do these annotations within the tool. Again, I recommend doing a few of your buy/sell analyses by hand so you can get a feel for the data.

Figure 19-1 Evaluation of Purchase and Sale of a Stock

If you had purchased XYZ, here's a possible timeline of your thoughts and comments:

- In late May, you purchased the stock for $30. You decided to set the Initial Purchase Stop Sell 6% below the Purchase Price of $30. Thirty dollars minus 6% is $28.20.

- In the next couple of days, the price dropped to $28.70. This was **not** low enough to trigger the Initial Purchase Stop Sell.

- In early June, the price rose to almost $33. Then it started to fall.

- At the end of June, the price fell below the Initial Purchase Stop Sell and triggered the sale of the stock at a loss.

- To add insult to injury, the price shot up to more than $35 during August.

In the bottom right-hand corner of the chart, you wrote a note to yourself, "Conclusion: If stop sell was 8% under, instead of 6%, would not have triggered." Does this mean that if you had set the Initial Purchase Stop Sell at 8%, XYZ would not have sold at a loss, and you would have enjoyed the profit that would have resulted from the price going higher than $35? In this case, yes. Does this mean that if you always set your Initial Purchase Stop Sell at 8% below the Purchase Price, you will never have a loss? I'm afraid not.

So, what's a Student of Commerce to do? Every time you do an analysis like this, you will learn something new. Investors have been trying for decades to create a formula or model that will predict exactly when to buy and sell stocks so that they never lose money and always make money. I don't mean to minimize the efforts of many brilliant men and women, but this sure-fire formula simply doesn't exist.

As an online investor, you have more tools at your fingertips than many professional stockbrokers did only a few years ago. The good news is that the stock market does move in trends and cycles. Every time you execute a transaction, you are adding to your knowledge base. Study your wins and celebrate. Study your losses even harder. When you see that you made a mistake, promise yourself, "I'll never do THAT again!"

Summary

- Keep all of your notes and research in a notebook.

- Have at least one page for each stock you own. As you get multiple pages of information about a stock, create separate sections for each one.

- Record free-form notes about each stock.

- Analyze each buy/sell transaction that you execute. Use the advantage of hindsight to conclude what you might do differently next time.

- Print out a historical price chart for each stock you buy and sell. Specify a time window that includes your Purchase Date and Sale Date.

- Mark up the price chart printout with your comments so that the graphical picture of your buy/sell experience also includes your conclusions.

20

Now, What Do I Do With All This Money?

Because you have read this book, at some point, you must have thought, "I WANT TO Make Money in the Stock Market." The last 19 chapters have given you the knowledge and tools to successfully begin your journey as a stock market investor. Using these tools, you will now be able to "...Make Money in the Stock Market."

"The only question with wealth is, what do you do with it?"

John D. Rockefeller (1839-1937) American Industrialist, Philanthropist, Founder of Exxon Mobil Corporation

With the tools presented in this book, you have the opportunity to earn quite a bit of money from your stock market investing. How much depends on lots of variables. Just a few of these are:

➢ How diligent you are in learning and applying the concepts in this book

➢ How much money you have to invest

➢ How well the economy is doing

➢ How well you apply the lessons you learn from your investing experience

➢ The length of time you invest your Hard-Earned Money.

Now if you make about $100 every month, that might pay for going out to eat and maybe a few movies. But let's daydream for a minute and consider what might happen if you make a bunch of money. What would you do if you started averaging an extra $500 per month? What would you do if you started averaging an extra $2,000 a month? How about $10,000?

You may have heard what happens to many people who win large amounts of money in a lottery. People that become overnight millionaires often have a wonderful time being extravagant and buying everything they ever wanted. The sobering statistics are that within a few years after their windfall, many have squandered their fortunes and are no better off than before their winnings. In fact, some are worse off. Why does this happen? The answer is simple. They didn't have a plan.

You need to have a plan

You need to have a financial plan for different levels of profit. You need a plan for having an extra $500 per month. You also need a $2,000 plan and a $10,000 plan. What if an unknown wealthy relative died and surprised you by leaving you a million dollars? Do you have a plan?

This is the fun part of being a Student of Commerce. It's free to dream, so dream big! You'll find that the more you dream, think, and plan a course of action, the more likely it will come to pass. Following is a short list of ideas you might want to incorporate into the different financial plans you will design. You'll be able to think of many more. Remember, it's free to dream!

Improve the health of your personal finances

One of the first areas of your personal finances that you want to attack is unsecured debt. Unsecured debt means that there is no corresponding asset to go with the financial liability. The liability of a home mortgage is offset by your home itself. The home is the corresponding asset that offsets the liability. Credit card debt is the major source of unsecured debt. What you paid for with a credit card may well have been eaten, worn out, lost, or discarded long ago. Yet you're still paying for it, **plus** interest. This is one of my favorite places to use the income from stock market investing. Every monthly payment that you eliminate is actually a lifetime raise that you give yourself!

Set up a contingency fund for life's unplanned expenses

I recommend that every family have a cash reserve. Experts suggest amounts that vary from a few hundred dollars to the equivalent of six months' salary. The point is, if you have some funds set aside, then when the hot water heater goes out or you have a fender bender, it doesn't hit the day-to-day cash flow so hard.

Be generous to your family, friends, and community

Almost everyone has had a season of hard financial times. As you begin to generate profits from investing, be on the lookout for times when you can be a hero to someone. A hundred dollars of groceries goes a long way to a family that is struggling with unemployment or illness. Paying the tuition for your niece's first semester at junior college may be the jump-start she needs to earn her university degree. There is no shortage of people with needs. Consider working generosity into each level of your financial plans.

Support a local ministry

The success of the stock market is built on the success of capitalism in America. The reason that capitalism is able to flourish is because of the foundational freedoms on which America was built. One of these core freedoms is the freedom of religion. The rich tapestry of life-giving ministries in America strengthens the social fabric that weaves us together. These ministries are responsible for promoting core moral values that make us better parents, neighbors, and businesspeople. If you're a member of a local ministry, consider making it part of your financial plan to generously support their programs. If you're not currently a member, you might want to give some of the ones in your community a fresh look. Many ministries near your home or workplace are working very hard to be responsive to your needs.

Write out your plan and update it regularly

Getting started is the most important part of creating a plan for using your increased finances. This can be as simple as writing on your notepad, "When I have an extra $500 per month, I'm going to spend it on..." You can add to your list and revise it for the rest of your life. Tear that piece of paper off the notepad and put it in your investing notebook. These creative thoughts will be the cornerstones of a more detailed plan later.

The future is in your hands!

Well done, Student of Commerce! You've completed this book and now have valuable tools at your command. I have confidence in your ability to use these tools in a most excellent manner to improve the quality of life for yourself and those around you. Enjoy the journey!

AFTERWORD

As you read through, <u>I WANT TO Make Money in the Stock Market</u>, you probably noticed several of the style strategies I employed:

- I used example dates that were far in the future.

- I used very few actual companies as examples.

- I didn't load the book with dozens of websites.

Example dates far in the future

I want this book to be a timeless reference for you. If this book has the long life that I hope it does, I don't want a date that is five years old make you feel like the information is dated. The concepts and principles I've outlined should last well into the 23rd Century!

Few actual companies as examples

HEYU is one of the fictitious companies referred to throughout the book. The reason that I used fictitious companies like HEYU is because I don't want someone to scan through the book and assume that I thought HEYU was a great investment. They might be tempted to buy stock in HEYU just because it was mentioned in the book. I wanted to teach you how to be a successful Student of Commerce. That means using the concepts and tools in the book to find your own Hockey Sticks and make your own decisions on where to spend your Hard-Earned Money.

Absence of website references

As you know, in today's fast-paced Internet society, online resources change quickly. Hundreds of websites start up and shut down daily. I didn't want to mention a website in the book only to have you go there and find that it no longer exists. Instead, I have directed you to the only website I can entrust you to...mine! The resources and links in <u>www.ChrisHart1.com</u> are ones that I personally use in my continuing education as a Student of Commerce. **I WANT TO** make these same resources available to you so that we can continue to grow together. I hope that you will visit me at <u>www.ChrisHart1.com</u> often.

A PERSONAL NOTE FROM CHRIS HART

I have enjoyed my journey as a Student of Commerce and have collected some excellent financial returns. There are also many other areas of my life where I have received rich blessings. My beautiful wife, Donna, and I have an exciting marriage, and I fall in love with her more every day. I have three wonderful sons who are working hard to create their own success in life. I have a beautiful home, great friends, and a loving extended family.

What I'd like to share with you is that none of these valuable riches in my life are the result of my own intelligence, creativity, or skill. When I tried to generate success by myself, I failed miserably. My efforts were usually shallow and self-centered. My life turned around when I paid attention to the fact that a religious figure I had heard about in Sunday School wanted to be my friend. It was an amazing revelation to find out that Jesus Christ was not only a historical icon, but because of the power of God, He is alive today. I was even more amazed to find out that He wanted to be a part of my life. Once I invited Jesus to be the Chief Executive Officer of my life, I found that for the first time, I had an accurate standard for Truth. I began to understand true morality, true friendship, and how to be true to my word.

Since I have asked Jesus into my life, I have made many mistakes. I have disappointed myself, my family, and my friends. What I learned in those dark times is that the whole reason God sent Jesus to earth is so that we could be forgiven. Receiving His forgiveness enabled me to receive the forgiveness of my family and friends.

The greatest gift I could offer you is to introduce you to The One who saved me from myself – Jesus Christ. Anything that is good in my life today is because I have turned my life over to Jesus. You can have this same valuable gift by asking. All you have to do is say out loud, in your own words, that you want Jesus to guide your life. If you ask Him, I promise that He will accept the challenge.

INDEX

Printed in the United States
39652LVS00003B/250-345

9 781598 002065